Study Guide for *Principles of Learning and Teaching,* 2nd Edition

► ► ► ► ► ► ► ► ► ► ►

A PUBLICATION OF EDUCATIONAL TESTING SERVICE

Table of Contents

Praxis Study Guide for the *Principles of Learning and Teaching* Tests

▶   ▶   ▶   ▶   ▶   ▶   ▶   ▶   ▶   ▶   ▶   ▶

TABLE OF CONTENTS

Chapter 1

Introduction to *Principles of Learning and Teaching* and
Suggestions for Using This Study Guide

▶ ▶ ▶ ▶ ▶ ▶ ▶ ▶ ▶ ▶ ▶ ▶

Introduction to *Principles of Learning and Teaching*

The *Principles of Learning and Teaching* tests are designed to assess a beginning teacher's knowledge of a broad range of job-related topics. Such knowledge is typically obtained in undergraduate courses in educational psychology, human growth and development, classroom management, instructional design and delivery techniques, evaluation and assessment, and other areas of professional preparation. Educational Testing Service (ETS) has aligned the content of this test with the principles developed by INTASC (Interstate New Teacher Assessment and Support Consortium) and published in the *INTASC Model Standards*. In developing assessment material for the *Principles of Learning and Teaching* test, ETS works in collaboration with teacher educators, higher education content specialists, and accomplished practicing teachers to keep the test updated and representative of current standards.

There are four different *Principles of Learning and Teaching* tests:

- *Principles of Learning and Teaching: Early Childhood*

- *Principles of Learning and Teaching: Grades K–6*

- *Principles of Learning and Teaching: Grades 5–9*

- *Principles of Learning and Teaching: Grades 7–12*

While the four tests cover the same fundamental topics and concepts, each test differs from the others by featuring developmentally appropriate cases and scenarios.

The format and contents of the test

Format

- Four case histories, each with three constructed-response questions

- Twenty-four discrete multiple-choice questions

Contents

Students as Learners (approximately 35% of total score)

- Student development and the learning process

- Students as diverse learners

- Student motivation and the learning environment

Instruction and Assessment (approximately 35% of total score)

- Instructional strategies

- Planning instruction

- Assessment strategies

Communication Techniques (approximately 15% of total score)

- Effective verbal and nonverbal communication

- Cultural and gender differences

- Stimulating discussion and responses in the classroom

Teacher Professionalism (approximately 15% of score)

- The reflective practitioner

- The larger community

Test takers have two hours to complete the test.

Suggestions for Using This Study Guide

Q. Why should you use this study guide?

This test is different from a final exam or other tests you may have taken for other courses, because it is comprehensive—that is, it covers material you may have learned in several courses during more than one year. It requires you to synthesize information you have learned from many sources and to understand the subject as a whole.

This test is very different from the SAT® or other assessments of your reading, writing, and mathematical skills. You may have heard it said that you can't study for the SAT—that you should have learned these skills throughout your school years, and you can't learn these skills just before you take the exam. You can *practice* taking the SAT and skills tests like it; you can become more adept at applying your reading, writing, and mathematical skills to the particular format of tests like the SAT.

However, the *Principles of Learning and Teaching* test assesses a domain of *knowledge* more than a set of skills. Therefore, you should review for and prepare for it, not merely practice with the question formats. A thorough review of the material covered on the test will significantly increase your likelihood of success.

Moreover, studying for your licensing exam is a great opportunity to reflect on and develop a deeper understanding of pedagogical knowledge and methods before you begin to teach. As you prepare to take the test, it may be particularly helpful for you to think about how you would apply the study topics and sample exercises to the clinical experience in schools that you obtained during your teacher preparation program. Your student teaching experience will be especially relevant to your thinking about the materials in the study guide.

Q. How can you best use the "Study Topics" chapter of this study guide?

All users of this book will probably want to begin with the following step:

- **Become familiar with the test content.** Learn what will be tested, as covered in chapter 3. It is quite likely that you will need to study in most or all of the areas. After you learn what the test contains, you should assess your knowledge in each area. How well do you know the material? In which areas do you need to learn more before you take the test?

Also, all users of this book will probably want to end with these two steps:

- **Familiarize yourself with test taking**. Chapter 8 is designed to answer frequently asked questions about the *Principles of Learning and Teaching* tests, such as whether it is a good idea to guess on a test. You can simulate the experience of the test by taking the practice test in chapter 6 (constructed-response) or chapter 9 (multiple-choice) within the specified time limits. Choose a time and place where you will not be interrupted or distracted. Then you can use chapter 7 to see sample responses to the constructed-response test and how they were scored; or you can use chapter 10 to score your multiple-choice responses. The scoring key in chapter 10 identifies which topic each question addresses, so you can see which areas are your strongest and weakest. Look over the explanations of the questions you missed and see whether you understand them and could answer similar questions correctly. Then plan any additional studying according to what you've learned about your understanding of the topics.

- **Register for the test and consider last-minute tips**. Review the checklist in chapter 11 to make sure you are ready for the test.

What you do between the first step and these last steps depends on whether you intend to use this book to prepare on your own or as part of a class or study group.

Using this book to prepare on your own:

If you are working by yourself to prepare for a *Principles of Learning and Teaching* test, you may find it helpful to use the following approach:

- **Fill out the Study Plan Sheet in appendix A.** This worksheet will help you to focus on what topics you need to study most, identify materials that will help you study, and set a schedule for doing the studying. The last item is particularly important if you know you tend to put off work.

- **Identify study materials.** Most of the material covered by the test is contained in standard introductory textbooks in the field. If you do not own introductory texts, you may want to borrow some from friends or from a library. Use standard introductory textbooks and other reliable, professionally prepared materials. Don't rely heavily on information provided by friends or from searching the World Wide Web. Neither of these sources is as uniformly reliable as textbooks.

- **Work through your study plan.** Work through the topics and questions provided in chapter 3. Be able to define and discuss the topics in your own words rather than memorizing definitions from books.

Using this book as part of a study group:

People who have a lot of studying to do sometimes find it helpful to form a study group with others who are preparing toward the same goal. Study groups give members opportunities to ask questions and get detailed answers. In a group, some members usually have a better understanding of certain topics, while others in the group may be better at other topics. As members take turns explaining concepts to each other, everyone builds self-confidence. If the group encounters a question that none of the members can answer well, the members can go as a group to a teacher or other expert and get answers efficiently. Because study groups schedule regular meetings, group members study in a more disciplined fashion. They also gain emotional support. The group should be large enough so that various people can contribute various kinds of knowledge, but small enough so that it stays focused. Often, three to six people is a good size.

Here are some ways to use this book as part of a study group:

- **Plan the group's study program.** Parts of the Study Plan Sheet in appendix A can help to structure your group's study program. By filling out the first five columns and sharing the work sheets, everyone will learn more about your group's mix of abilities and about the resources (such as textbooks) that members can share with the group. In the sixth column ("Dates planned for study of content"), you can create an overall schedule for your group's study program.

- **Plan individual group sessions.** At the end of each session, the group should decide what specific topics will be covered at the next meeting and who will be the presenter of each topic. Use the topic headings and subheadings in chapter 3 to select topics. Some sessions might be based on the topics outlined in these chapters; other sessions might be based on the questions from these chapters.

- **Prepare your presentation for the group.** When it's your turn to be presenter, prepare something that's more than a lecture. If you are presenting material from chapter 3, write five to ten original questions to pose to the group. Practicing writing actual questions can help you better understand the topics covered on the test as well as the types of questions you will encounter on the test. It will also give other members of the group extra practice at answering questions. If you are presenting material from the sample questions, use each sample question as a model for writing at least one original question.

■ **Take the practice tests together.** The idea of chapters 6 and 9 is to simulate actual administrations of the test, so scheduling a test session with the group will add to the realism and will also help boost everyone's confidence.

■ **Learn from the results of the practice test.** Use chapter 7 or chapter 10 to score each other's answer sheets. Then plan one or more study sessions based on the questions that group members got wrong or (on the constructed-response sample test) did not answer well. For example, each group member might be responsible for a question that he or she got wrong and could use it as a model to create an original question to pose to the group, together with an explanation of the correct answer modeled after the explanations in chapter 10.

Whether you decide to study alone or with a group, remember that the best way to prepare is to have an organized plan. The plan should set goals based on specific topics and skills that you need to learn, and it should commit you to a realistic set of deadlines for meeting these goals. Then you need to discipline yourself to stick with your plan and accomplish your goals on schedule.

Q. What's the best way to use the chapters on case studies and multiple-choice questions?

■ **Become familiar with case studies.** Learn what a case study is and how to read one carefully and analytically in preparation for answering questions about it. This is covered in chapter 4. Think about possible applications of situations and issues in the case studies to your own teaching experience. What information does your own teaching background provide for answering the questions?

■ **Sharpen your skills on short-answer questions.** Read chapter 5 to understand how short-answer questions are scored and how to write high-scoring responses.

■ **Read chapter 8.** This chapter will sharpen your skills in reading and answering multiple-choice questions. Succeeding on multiple-choice questions requires careful focus on the question, attention to detail, and patient sifting of the answer choices.

Q. What's the best way to use the practice-test chapters?

- **Answer the short-answer questions.** Work on the practice cases and short-answer questions in chapter 6, then review the scoring materials and sample responses in chapter 7.

- **Answer the practice multiple-choice questions.** Work on the practice questions in chapter 9, then go through the detailed answers in chapter 10 and mark the questions you answered correctly and the ones you missed. Look over the explanations of the questions you missed and see if you understand them.

- **Decide whether you need more review.** After you have looked at your results, decide if there are areas that you need to brush up on before taking the actual test. Go back to your textbooks and reference materials to see if the topics are covered there. You might also want to go over your questions with a friend or teacher who is familiar with the subjects.

- **Assess your readiness.** Do you feel confident about your level of understanding in each of the subject areas? If not, where do you need more work? If you feel ready, complete the checklist in chapter 11 to double-check that you've thought through the details. If you need more information about registration or the testing situation itself, use the resources in appendix B: "For More Information."

Chapter 2

Background Information on
The Praxis Series™ Assessments

▶ ▶ ▶ ▶ ▶ ▶ ▶ ▶ ▶ ▶ ▶ ▶

What Are The Praxis Series Subject Assessments?

The Praxis Series™ Subject Assessments are designed by Educational Testing Service (ETS) to assess your knowledge of the subject area you plan to teach, and they are a part of the licensing procedure in many states. This study guide covers an assessment that tests your knowledge of the actual content you hope to be licensed to teach. Your state has adopted The Praxis Series tests because it wants to be certain that you have achieved a specified level of mastery of your subject area before it grants you a license to teach in a classroom.

The Praxis Series tests are part of a national testing program, meaning that the test covered in this study guide is used in more than one state. The advantage of taking Praxis tests is that if you want to move to another state that uses The Praxis Series tests, you can transfer your scores to that state. Passing scores are set by states, however, so if you are planning to apply for licensure in another state, you may find that passing scores are different. You can find passing scores for all states that use The Praxis Series tests in the *Understanding Your Praxis Scores* pamphlet, available online at www.ets.org/praxis, in your college's School of Education, or by calling 800-772-9476 or 609-771-7395.

What Is Licensure?

Licensure in any area—medicine, law, architecture, accounting, cosmetology—is an assurance to the public that the person holding the license has demonstrated a certain level of competence. The phrase used in licensure is that the person holding the license *will do no harm*. In the case of teacher licensing, a license tells the public that the person holding the license can be trusted to educate children competently and professionally.

Because a license makes such a serious claim about its holder, licensure tests are usually quite demanding. In some fields licensure tests have more than one part and last for more than one day. Candidates for licensure in all fields plan intensive study as part of their professional preparation: some join study groups, others study alone. But preparing to take a licensure test is, in all cases, a professional activity. Because it assesses your entire body of knowledge or skill for the field you want to enter, preparing for a licensure exam takes planning, discipline, and sustained effort. Studying thoroughly is highly recommended.

Why Does My State Require The Praxis Series Assessments?

Your state chose The Praxis Series Assessments because the tests assess the breadth and depth of content— called the "domain" of the test—that your state wants its teachers to possess before they begin to teach. The level of content knowledge, reflected in the passing score, is based on recommendations of panels of teachers and teacher educators in each subject area in each state. The state licensing agency and, in some states, the state legislature ratify the passing scores that have been recommended by panels of teachers. You can find out the passing score required for The Praxis Series Assessments in your state by looking in the pamphlet *Understanding Your Praxis Scores*, which is free from ETS (see above). If you look through this pamphlet, you will see that not all states use the same test modules, and even when they do, the passing scores can differ from state to state.

What Kinds of Tests Are The Praxis Series Subject Assessments?

Two kinds of tests comprise The Praxis Series Subject Assessments: multiple-choice (for which you select your answer from a list of choices) and constructed-response (for which you write a response of your own). Multiple-choice tests can survey a wider domain because they can ask more questions in a limited period of time. Constructed-response tests have far fewer questions, but the questions require you to demonstrate the depth of your knowledge in the area covered.

What Do the Tests Measure?

The Praxis Series Subject Assessments are tests of content knowledge. They measure your understanding of the subject area you want to teach. The multiple-choice tests measure a broad range of knowledge across your content area. The constructed-response tests measure your ability to explain in depth a few essential topics in your subject area. The content-specific pedagogy tests, most of which are constructed-response, measure your understanding of how to teach certain fundamental concepts in your field. The tests do not measure your actual teaching ability, however. They measure your knowledge of your subject and of how to teach it. The teachers in your field who help us design and write these tests, and the states that require these tests, do so in the belief that knowledge of subject area is the first requirement for licensing. Your teaching ability is a skill that is measured in other ways: observation, videotaped teaching, or portfolios are typically used by states to measure teaching ability. Teaching combines many complex skills, only some of which can be measured by a single test. The Praxis Series Subject Assessments are designed to measure how thoroughly you understand the material in the subject areas in which you want to be licensed to teach.

How Were These Tests Developed?

ETS began the development of The Praxis Series Subject Assessments with a survey. For each subject, teachers around the country in various teaching situations were asked to judge which knowledge and skills a beginning teacher in that subject needs to possess. Professors in schools of education who prepare teachers were asked the same questions. These responses were ranked in order of importance and sent out to hundreds of teachers for review. All of the responses to these surveys (called "job analysis surveys") were analyzed to summarize the judgments of these professionals. From their consensus, we developed the specifications for the multiple-choice and constructed-response tests. Each subject area had a committee of practicing teachers and teacher educators who wrote these specifications (guidelines). The specifications were reviewed and eventually approved by teachers. From the test specifications, groups of teachers and professional test developers created test questions.

When your state adopted The Praxis Series Subject Assessments, local panels of practicing teachers and teacher educators in each subject area met to examine the tests question by question and evaluate each question for its relevance to beginning teachers in your state. This is called a "validity study." A test is considered "valid" for a job if it measures what people must know and be able to do on that job. For the test to be adopted in your state, teachers in your state must judge that it is valid.

These teachers and teacher educators also performed a "standard-setting study"; that is, they went through the tests question by question and decided, through a rigorous process, how many questions a beginning teacher would be able to answer correctly. From this study emerged a recommended passing score. The final passing score was approved by your state's licensing agency.

In other words, throughout the development process, practitioners in the teaching field—teachers and teacher educators—have determined what the tests would contain. The practitioners in your state determined which tests would be used for licensure in your subject area and helped decide what score would be needed to achieve licensure. This is how professional licensure works in most fields: those who are already licensed oversee the licensing of new practitioners. When you pass The Praxis Series Subject Assessments, you and the practitioners in your state can be assured that you have the knowledge required to begin practicing your profession.

Chapter 3
Study Topics

▶ ▶ ▶ ▶ ▶ ▶ ▶ ▶ ▶ ▶ ▶ ▶

Introduction to the Test

The *Principles of Learning and Teaching* tests are designed to evaluate the professional knowledge of beginning teachers. They are closely aligned with the national standards for what teachers should know and be able to do that have been written and adopted by states in the INTASC (Interstate New Teacher Assessment and Support Consortium). The second part of this chapter directly compares the INTASC standards with the topics covered on this test, showing what parts of the standards are and are not covered in the test, with accompanying explanations.

The tests require you to respond in two different ways. Some of the questions are constructed-response questions and require you to write out your answers. Others are multiple-choice and require you to select an answer from a set of four options. For both parts of each test, you will need to apply knowledge about teaching that you have gained from your course work and field work such as student teaching. This chapter is intended to help you organize your preparation for your test and to give you a clear indication about the depth and breadth of the knowledge required for success on the tests.

Here is an overview of the areas of knowledge covered in the *Principles of Learning and Teaching* tests:

Students as Learners
> **Student development and the learning process**
> **Students as diverse learners**
> **Student motivation and the learning environment**

Instruction and Assessment
> **Instructional strategies**
> **Planning instruction**
> **Assessment strategies**

Communication Techniques
> **Effective verbal and nonverbal communication**
> **Cultural and gender differences in communication**
> **Stimulating discussion and responses in the classroom**

Profession and Community
> **The reflective practitioner**
> **The larger community**

Using the topic lists that follow. You are not expected to be an expert on the topics that follow. But you should understand the major characteristics or aspects of each topic and be able to relate the topic to various situations presented in the test questions. For instance, here is one of the topic lists in "Instructional Strategies," under the "Instruction and Assessment" category:

▶ Major categories of instructional strategies, including

- Cooperative learning

- Direct instruction

- Discovery learning

- Whole-group discussion

- Independent study

- Interdisciplinary instruction

- Concept mapping

- Inquiry method

- Questioning

Using textbooks and other sources as needed, make sure you can describe each of these strategies in your own words. Find materials that will help you identify examples of each and situations for which each is appropriate. On the test you may be asked direct questions on one or more of these topics, or you may be asked to evaluate the use or appropriateness of a strategy in a particular context.

Special questions marked with stars. Interspersed throughout the list of topics are questions that are outlined in boxes and preceded by stars (☆). These questions are intended to help you test your knowledge of fundamental concepts and your ability to apply fundamental concepts to typical classroom situations. Most of the questions require you to combine several pieces of knowledge in order to formulate an integrated understanding and response. If you spend time on these questions, you will gain increased understanding and facility with the subject matter covered on the test. You might want to discuss these questions and your answers with a teacher or mentor.

Note that the questions marked with stars are not short-answer or multiple-choice. The questions marked with stars are intended as *study* questions, not practice questions. Thinking about the answers to them should improve your understanding of fundamental concepts and will probably help you answer a broad range of questions on the test. For example, the following box with a star appears in the list of study topics under "Planning Instruction."

If you think about the relationships among curriculum goals, scope and sequence frameworks, and unit and lesson plans, you have probably prepared yourself to answer multiple-choice questions similar to the one below, which asks you to link a curricular goal with the most appropriate performance objective.

The goal of a particular mathematics curriculum is for students to use computational strategies fluently and estimate appropriately. Which of the following objectives for students best reflects that goal?

(A) Students in all grades will use calculators for all mathematical tasks.

(B) Students in all grades will be drilled daily on basic number facts.

(C) Students in all grades will know the connections between the basic arithmetic operations.

(D) Students in all grades will evaluate the reasonableness of their answers.

(The correct answer is (D). To "evaluate the reasonableness of their answers," students must understand the computational strategies involved in mathematical solutions before they are able to estimate or to evaluate estimated answers.)

Teachers are responsible for connecting scope and sequence frameworks and curriculum goals into classroom lessons and groups of lessons. How does a teacher translate curriculum goals and discipline-specific scope and sequence frameworks into unit and lesson plans with objectives, activities, and assessments appropriate for the students being taught? Give an example of a curriculum goal and then write a lesson objective, one activity, and an idea for an assessment of student learning that would accomplish that goal.

Students as Learners

Student development and the learning process

You will notice that in this section, the names of important theorists appear in more than one category. This is because the work of these theorists has implications for multiple domains that are important to effective teaching

▶ Theoretical foundations about how learning occurs: how students construct knowledge, acquire skills, and develop habits of mind

▶ Examples of important theorists

- Albert Bandura
- Jerome Bruner
- John Dewey
- Jean Piaget
- Lev Vygotsky
- Howard Gardner
- Abraham Maslow
- B. F. Skinner

☆ Knowing each theorist's major ideas and being able to compare and contrast one theory with another comprises basic professional knowledge for teachers. In addition, knowing how these ideas actually can be applied to teaching practice is important professional knowledge for teachers.

☆ What are the major differences between Jerome Bruner's and Jean Piaget's theories of cognitive development in young children?

☆ How might a teacher apply some of Lev Vygotsky's ideas about scaffolding and direct instruction in the classroom?

☆ What does Gardner's work on multiple intelligences suggest about planning instruction?

☆ What does Abraham Maslow's hierarchy of needs suggest about motivation for learning in the classroom?

▸ Important terms that relate to learning theory

- Constructivism
- Metacognition
- Readiness
- Schemata
- Transfer
- Scaffolding
- Bloom's taxonomy
- Zone of proximal development
- Intrinsic and extrinsic motivation

▸ Human development in the physical, social, emotional, moral, and cognitive domains

- The theoretical contributions of important theorists such as Erik Erikson, Lawrence Kohlberg, Carol Gilligan, Jean Piaget, Abraham Maslow, Albert Bandura, and Lev Vygotsky

- The major progressions in each developmental domain and the ranges of individual variation within each domain

- The impact of students' physical, social, emotional, moral, and cognitive development on their learning and how to address these factors when making instructional decisions

- How development in one domain, such as physical, may affect performance in another domain, such as social

☆ Go beyond memorization of definitions; try to apply the terms to the theories behind them and think of applications in the classroom.

☆ What are some specific classroom-based examples of extrinsic and intrinsic motivators for students?

☆ Make sure you can recognize the differences between lower-order and higher-order thinking in classroom activities, using Bloom's taxonomy as a guide.

☆ What is an example of a schema and what good is it?

☆ What is scaffolding and why is it important for both teachers and students?

☆ When responding to case studies, you will be asked to perform the following kinds of tasks related to the area of human development and the learning process:

Identify and describe strengths and/or weaknesses in

- the instruction described in the case, in terms of its appropriateness for students at a particular age

Propose a strategy for

- instruction that would be appropriate for students at the age described in the case

Give a specific example from your own classroom experience of the effects of differences in learning styles on how people understand and express what they know.

What is an example of the way cultural expectations from a particular geographical region or ethnic group might affect how students learn or express what they know?

What does the research reveal about gender differences and how they might affect learning?

Know the major types of challenges in each category (e.g., dyslexia under "Learning Disabilities"), know the major symptoms and range of severity, and know the major classroom and instructional issues related to each area.

Know the basic rights or responsibilities that the legislation established.

Students as diverse learners

▶ Differences in the ways students learn and perform

- Learning styles
- Multiple intelligences
- Performance modes
  — Concrete operational thinkers
  — Visual and aural learners
- Gender differences
- Cultural expectations and styles

▶ Areas of exceptionality in student learning

- Visual and perceptual difficulties
- Special physical or sensory challenges
- Learning disabilities
- Attention Deficit Disorder (ADD); Attention Deficit-Hyperactivity Disorder (ADHD)
- Functional mental retardation
- Behavioral disorders
- Developmental delays

▶ Legislation and institutional responsibilities relating to exceptional students:

- Americans with Disabilities Act (ADA)
- Individuals with Disabilities Education Act (IDEA)
- Inclusion, mainstreaming, and "Least Restrictive Environment"
- IEP (Individual Education Plan), including what, by law, must be included in each IEP
- Section 504 of the Rehabilitation Act
- Due process
- Family involvement

▶ Approaches for accommodating various learning styles, intelligences, or exceptionalities, including:

- Differentiated instruction
- Alternative assessments
- Testing modifications

▶ The process of second language acquisition, and strategies to support the learning of students for whom English is not a first language

▶ How students' learning is influenced by individual experiences, talents, and prior learning, as well as language, culture, family, and community values, including:

- Multicultural backgrounds

- Age-appropriate knowledge and behavior

- The student culture at the school

- Family backgrounds

- Linguistic patterns and differences

- Cognitive patterns and differences

- Social and emotional issues

When responding to case studies, you will be asked to perform the following kinds of tasks related to the area of students as diverse learners:

Identify and describe a strength and/or weakness in

- a lesson plan for meeting needs of individual students with identified special needs, as described in the case

- the interaction described in the case between the teacher and students in terms of culturally responsive teaching

Propose a strategy for

- helping the students with attention deficit problems described in the case stay on task (e.g., in listening to a lecture, following a demonstration, doing written work)

- improving performance of students in the case who do not perform well on homework, original compositions, or other assignments

- helping students in the case for whom English is not the first language build literacy skills and/or improve in academic areas

- meeting the needs of a wide range of students (especially students with learning difficulties and students who are accelerated)

- building positive relationships with a student the case shows is very turned off to school

- adapting instruction and/or assessment for an individual student with identified needs described in the case

- helping the students described in the case see issues from different points of view

Student motivation and the learning environment

▶ Theoretical foundations about human motivation and behavior

- Abraham Maslow
- Albert Bandura
- B. F. Skinner

▶ Important terms that relate to motivation and behavior

- Hierarchy of needs
- Correlational and causal relationships
- Intrinsic motivation
- Extrinsic motivation
- Learned helplessness
- Self-efficacy
- Operant conditioning
- Reinforcement
- Positive reinforcement
- Negative reinforcement
- Shaping successive approximations
- Prevention
- Extinction
- Punishment
- Continuous reinforcement
- Intermittent reinforcement

▶ How knowledge of human motivation and behavior should influence strategies for organizing and supporting individual and group work in the classroom

▶ Factors and situations that are likely to promote or diminish students' motivation to learn; how to help students become self-motivated

☆ Go beyond memorization of definitions; try to apply the terms to the theories behind them and think of applications in the teaching situation.

▶ Principles of effective classroom management and strategies to promote positive relationships, cooperation, and purposeful learning, including:

- Establishing daily procedures and routines

- Establishing classroom rules

- Using natural and logical consequences

- Providing positive guidance

- Modeling conflict resolution, problem solving, and anger management

- Giving timely feedback

- Maintaining accurate records

- Communicating with parents and caregivers

- Using objective behavior descriptions

- Responding to student misbehavior

- Arranging of classroom space

- Pacing and structuring the lesson

☆ Why is each of the principles to the left a good practice for teachers to cultivate and maintain in terms of its effect on student learning? How can each help you to be a more effective teacher? What are the characteristics of effective implementation of each of these practices? How can you structure your instructional planning to include these?

☆ What are the choices a teacher has in each of the last three bulleted items to the left? What are the most important considerations when making decisions about each one?

☆ Pacing and structuring of a lesson is a particularly challenging aspect of instruction. What factors can change the pace and structure of a lesson as it unfolds? How can you prepare *in advance* for adjusting the pace and the structure of a lesson for each of these factors?

☆ When responding to case studies, you will be asked to perform the following kinds of tasks related to the area of student motivation and the learning environment:

Propose a strategy for

- revising a lesson that is described in the case for improving student engagement and motivation

- improving motivation through means other than negative strategies described in the case

- addressing behavioral problems that are described in the case

Identify and describe a strength and/or weakness in

- a lesson plan or instructional strategy described in the case with the intention of building a positive classroom environment

Instruction and Assessment

Instructional strategies

What are some specific instructional goals in a particular content area that would be associated with each of these cognitive processes?

How are these cognitive processes connected with the developmental level of students?

How are these processes different from each other?

What are some ways that teachers can stimulate each of these cognitive processes in a lesson?

What are the primary advantages of each of these strategies? In general terms, describe the kinds of situations or the kinds of goals and objectives for which each of these strategies is appropriate. What kinds of information about students' learning styles and achievement levels does each of these offer? When would you NOT use a particular instructional strategy?

▶ The major cognitive processes associated with student learning, including:

- Critical thinking
- Creative thinking
- Higher-order thinking
- Inductive and deductive thinking
- Problem-structuring and problem-solving
- Invention
- Memorization and recall
- Social reasoning
- Representation of ideas

▶ Major categories of instructional strategies, including:

- Cooperative learning
- Direct instruction
- Discovery learning
- Whole-group discussion
- Independent study
- Interdisciplinary instruction
- Concept mapping
- Inquiry method
- Questioning
- Play
- Learning centers
- Small group work
- Revisiting
- Reflection
- Project approach

▶ Principles, techniques, and methods associated with various instructional strategies, including:

- Direct instruction
  - Madeline Hunter's "Effective Teaching Model"
  - David Ausubel's "Advance Organizers"
  - Mastery learning
  - Demonstrations
  - Mnemonics
  - Note-taking
  - Outlining
  - Use of visual aids
- Student-centered models
  - Inquiry model
  - Discovery learning
  - Cooperative learning (pair-share, jigsaw, STAD, teams, games, tournaments)
  - Collaborative learning
  - Concept models (concept development, concept attainment, concept mapping)
  - Discussion models
  - Laboratories
  - Project-based learning
  - Simulations

☆ What are some examples of appropriate situations for grouping students heterogeneously? What are some for grouping students homogeneously? Besides grouping by performance level, what are other characteristics that a teacher should sometimes consider when grouping students?

☆ What is wait-time? What does research suggest about wait-time?

☆ How might a teacher promote critical thinking among students in a discussion?

☆ How can a teacher encourage student-to-student dialogue in a class discussion?

☆ What kinds of classroom management procedures and rules would tend to make class discussion more productive?

☆ How does the developmental level of students affect the way a teacher might handle classroom discussion?

☆ In what kinds of discussions or situations should a teacher name a specific student before asking a question? When is it best *not* to name a specific student?

Instructional strategies (continued)

▶ Methods for enhancing student learning through the use of a variety of resources and materials

- Computers, Internet resources, Web pages, e-mail
- Audio-visual technologies such as videotapes and compact discs
- Local experts
- Primary documents and artifacts
- Field trips
- Libraries
- Service learning

☆ What should a teacher consider when planning to incorporate various resources into a lesson design?

☆ What are the advantages of these different resources?

☆ When responding to case studies, you will be asked to perform the following kinds of tasks related to the area of instructional planning:

Identify and describe a strength and/or weakness in

- specific activities that are described in the case

Propose a strategy for

- teaching critical thinking skills in a specific lesson described in the case
- achieving effectiveness with group work in a particular situation described in the case
- helping students stay on task in the situation described in the case
- helping students learn material presented through various media introduced in the case
- assigning students to group work appropriate to the case
- bringing closure to a lesson that stops abruptly as presented in the case
- improving student interaction during class discussion as described in the case
- addressing a "missed opportunity" during instruction that is described in the case

Planning instruction

▶ Techniques for planning instruction to meet curriculum goals, including the incorporation of learning theory, subject matter, curriculum development, and student development

- National and state learning standards
- State and local curriculum frameworks
- State and local curriculum guides
- Scope and sequence in specific disciplines
- Units and lessons—rationale for selecting content topics
- Behavioral objectives: affective, cognitive, psychomotor
- Learner objectives and outcomes
- Emergent curriculum
- Anti-bias curriculum
- Themes/projects
- Curriculum webbing

▶ Techniques for creating effective bridges between curriculum goals and students' experiences

- Modeling
- Guided practice
- Independent practice, including homework
- Transitions

☆ Teachers are responsible for connecting scope and sequence frameworks and curriculum goals into classroom lessons and groups of lessons. How does a teacher translate curriculum goals and discipline-specific scope and sequence frameworks into unit and lesson plans with objectives, activities, and assessments appropriate for the students being taught? Give an example of a curriculum goal and then write a lesson objective, one activity, and an idea for an assessment of student learning that would accomplish that goal.

☆ How do behavioral objectives and learner objectives and outcomes fit into a teacher's planning for units and lessons?

☆ What criterion or criteria does a teacher use to decide when to use each of these techniques?

☆ Why is it so important for a teacher to plan carefully for transitions? What are the risks if transitions are not thought through and executed with care?

Planning instruction (continued)

- Activating students' prior knowledge
- Anticipating preconceptions
- Encouraging exploration and problem-solving
- Building new skills on those previously acquired
- Predicting

☆ Why is each of these actions a principle of effective instruction?

☆ What tools and techniques can a teacher plan to use to accomplish each one?

☆ What strategies can a teacher employ to monitor student understanding as a lesson unfolds?

☆ What evidence should the teacher observe in order to know whether to re-teach a topic, move more quickly, or go back to material previously covered?

☆ When responding to case studies, you will be asked to perform the following kinds of tasks related to the area of instructional planning:

Identify and describe a strength and/or weakness in

- a unit plan that is described in the case
- specific strategies used in instruction (e.g., using lecture, using class discussion) in the case
- a sequence of lessons described in the case designed to achieve a goal or set of objectives
- one or more written assignments given to students in the case

Propose a strategy for

- meeting what may appear to be conflicting goals or objectives described in the case
- incorporating activities that will have students described in the case draw on their own experiences to understand the instruction
- stimulating prior knowledge in the situation described in the case

Assessment strategies

▶ Measurement theory and assessment-related issues

- Types of assessments
  - Standardized tests, norm-referenced or criterion-referenced
  - Achievement tests
  - Aptitude tests
  - Structured observations
  - Anecdotal notes
  - Assessments of prior knowledge
  - Student responses during a lesson
  - Portfolios
  - Essays written to prompts
  - Journals
  - Self-evaluations
  - Performance assessments

- Characteristics of assessments
  - Validity
  - Reliability
  - Norm-referenced
  - Criterion-referenced
  - Mean, median, mode
  - Sampling strategy

- Scoring assessments
  - Analytical scoring
  - Holistic scoring
  - Rubrics
  - Reporting assessment results
    - Percentile rank
    - Stanines
    - Mastery levels

continued on next page

☆ What are the characteristics, uses, advantages, and limitations of each of the formal and informal types of assessments to the left?

☆ When might you use "holistic scoring?"

☆ Under what circumstances would "anecdotal notes" give a teacher important assessment information?

☆ How might a teacher effectively use student self-evaluations?

☆ What are some examples of informal assessments of prior knowledge that a teacher can easily use when a new topic is introduced?

☆ What kind of assessment information can a teacher gather from student journals?

☆ What is a structured observation in a classroom setting?

When responding to case studies, you will be asked to perform the following types of tasks related to the area of assessment:

Propose a strategy for

- assessing progress for students described in the case who are working toward specified goals or objectives

- assessing class progress toward achievement of specified goals or objectives

- gathering information to use to help understand classroom performance that is different from what was expected at the beginning of the year

- assessing language fluency of a student for whom English is not the first language

Propose a hypothesis or explanation for

- a student's strengths and/or weaknesses as a learner based on the evidence presented

- what might be important to explore in working with a student described in the case who is having difficulties academically, socially, or emotionally

Assessment strategies (continued)

Raw score

Scaled score

Grade equivalent score

Standard deviation

Standard error of measurement

- Uses of assessments

    — Formative evaluation

    — Summative evaluation

    — Diagnostic evaluation

- Understanding measurement theory and assessment-related issues

- Interpreting and communicating results of assessments

Communication Techniques

▶ Basic, effective verbal and nonverbal communication techniques

▶ The effect of cultural and gender differences on communications in the classroom

☆ What are some ways that a teacher's raising his or her voice might be interpreted differently by students with different cultural backgrounds?

☆ What are specific examples of gestures and other body language that have different meanings in different cultures? (For example, looking someone directly in the eye, disagreeing openly during a discussion, pointing)

▶ Types of questions that can stimulate discussion in different ways for particular purposes

- Probing for learner understanding
- Helping students articulate their ideas and thinking processes
- Promoting risk-taking and problem-solving
- Facilitating factual recall
- Encouraging convergent and divergent thinking
- Stimulating curiosity
- Helping students to question
- Promoting a caring community

☆ What is an example of a question in a particular content area that probes for understanding?

☆ What is an example of a question that would help a student articulate his or her ideas?

☆ What is an example of a comment a teacher might make that would promote risk-taking? Problem-solving?

☆ How would a teacher encourage divergent thinking on a particular topic?

☆ How would a teacher encourage students to question each other and the teacher?

When responding to case studies, you will be asked to perform the following kinds of tasks related to the area of communication:

Identify and describe a strength and/or weakness in

- the teacher's oral or written communication with students in the case (e.g., feedback on assignments, interaction during class)

Propose a strategy for

- improving the self-image of a student described in the case or the student's sense of responsibility for his or her own learning

- involving all students in a class discussion described in the case in a positive way, showing respect for others

- helping a student described in the case to develop social skills in a specified situation

Profession and Community

The reflective practitioner

▸ Types of resources available for professional development and learning

- Professional literature
- Colleagues
- Professional associations
- Professional development activities

▸ Ability to read, understand, and apply articles and books about current research, views, ideas, and debates regarding best teaching practices

▸ Why personal reflection on teaching practices is critical, and approaches that can be used to reflect and evaluate

- Code of ethics
- Advocacy for learners

The larger community

▸ The role of the school as a resource to the larger community

- Teachers as a resource

▸ Factors in the students' environment outside of school (family circumstances, community environments, health and economic conditions) that may influence students' life and learning

▸ Basic strategies for developing and utilizing active partnerships among teachers, parents/guardians, and leaders in the community to support the educational process

- Shared ownership
- Shared decision making
- Respectful/reciprocal communication

☆ Be able to read and understand articles and books about current views, ideas, and debates regarding best teaching practices.

☆ What types of help or learning can each of these resources offer a new teacher?

☆ What are the titles of two professional journals of particular interest to you in your chosen field of teaching that you might subscribe to?

☆ What is/are the professional association(s) that offer professional meetings and publications and opportunities for collaborative conversation with other teachers?

☆ What might be a professional development plan for the first two years of a teacher's career that would support his or her learning and growth?

When responding to case studies, you will be asked to perform the following kinds of tasks related to the area of the larger community:

Identify and describe a strength and/or weakness in

- the communication with parents used by a teacher described in the case

- the approach used by a teacher described in the case to involve parents

Propose a strategy for

- using parent volunteers during a lesson that is described in a case

- involving all parents or other caregivers in helping students in areas specified in the case

- helping the family of a student described in the case work with the student's learning or other needs

Major laws related to students' rights and teacher responsibilities

- Equal education

- Appropriate education for students with special needs

- Confidentiality and privacy

- Appropriate treatment of students

- Reporting in situations related to possible child abuse

Comparison of the *Principles of Learning and Teaching* Test Topics and the INTASC *Model Standards*

The *Principles of Learning and Teaching* tests are closely aligned with the INTASC *Model Standards,* as the pages that follow demonstrate. However, the INTASC *Model Standards* describe the entire domain of teaching, what teachers should know ("knowledge"), how they should think and act ("dispositions"), and what they can and should be able to do ("performances"). The *Principles of Learning and Teaching* tests focus on what beginning teachers should know and do not assess a teacher's actual behavior in the classroom. In some instances, however, the tests require evaluation of teacher performance described in a case study. This offers assessment of many of the "performance" aspects covered in the INTASC standards, though not a direct assessment of the test-takers' actual performance on the job.

In the pages that follow, you will see the actual language of the INTASC *Model Standards* linked to the content of the *Principles of Learning and Teaching* tests. Aspects of the INTASC standards that are not covered in the test—mostly in the "dispositions" category—are shaded.

Principles of Learning and Teaching Test Topics

INTASC Standards

This category is not included in the *Principles of Learning and Teaching* tests	**Principle 1: The teacher understands the central concepts, tools of inquiry, and structures of the discipline(s) he or she teaches and can create learning experiences that make these aspects of subject matter meaningful for students.**

INTASC Principle 1 focuses on teachers' knowledge, dispositions, and performances in a *particular subject area.* In The Praxis Series Assessments, specific knowledge in the academic disciplines is covered in other tests. The *Principles of Learning and Teaching* tests are intentionally free of questions probing knowledge about particular subjects and content-specific pedagogy. The intent of the *Principles of Learning and Teaching* tests is to test concepts and methods that cut across discipline boundaries. Therefore, the first INTASC standard is not assessed by the *Principles of Learning and Teaching* tests.

Knowledge

The teacher understands major concepts, assumptions, debates, processes of inquiry, and ways of knowing that are central to the discipline(s) she or he teaches.

The teacher understands how students' conceptual frameworks and misconceptions for an area of knowledge can influence their learning.

The teacher can relate his/her disciplinary knowledge to other subject areas.

Dispositions

The teacher realizes that subject matter knowledge is not a fixed body of facts but is complex and ever-evolving. S/he seeks to keep abreast of new ideas and understandings in the field.

Shaded means that the standard is not covered in the *Principles of Learning and Teaching* tests.

Principles of Learning and Teaching Test Topics

INTASC *Standards*

This category is not included in the *Principles of Learning and Teaching* tests	Principle 1: The teacher understands the central concepts, tools of inquiry, and structures of the discipline(s) he or she teaches and can create learning experiences that make these aspects of subject matter meaningful for students.
	Performances The teacher effectively uses multiple representations and explanations of disciplinary concepts that capture key ideas and links them to students' prior understanding. The teacher can represent and use differing viewpoints, theories, "ways of knowing," and methods of inquiry in his/her teaching of subject matter concepts. The teacher can evaluate teaching resources and curriculum materials for comprehensiveness, accuracy, and usefulness for representing particular ideas and concepts. The teacher engages students in generating knowledge and testing hypotheses according to the methods of inquiry and standards of evidence used in the discipline. The teacher develops and uses curricula that encourage students to see, question, and interpret ideas from diverse perspectives. The teacher can create interdisciplinary learning experiences that allow students to integrate knowledge, skills, and methods of inquiry from several subject areas.

Shaded means that the standard is not covered in the *Principles of Learning and Teaching* tests.

Principles of Learning and Teaching Test Topics

INTASC *Standards*

Student development and the learning process	**Principle 2: The teacher understands how children learn and develop, and can provide learning opportunities that support their intellectual, social and personal development.**

Knowledge

➤ Theoretical foundations about how learning occurs: how students construct knowledge, acquire skills, and develop habits of mind

- Important theorists and theories
- Important concepts

➤ Human development in the physical, social, emotional, moral, and cognitive domains

- Important theorists and theories
- The major progressions in each developmental domain and the ranges of individual variation within each domain
- The impact of students' physical, social, emotional, moral, and cognitive development on their learning and how to address these factors when making instructional decisions
- How development in one domain, such as physical, may affect performance in another domain, such as social

The teacher understands how learning occurs— how students construct knowledge, acquire skills, and develop habits of mind—and knows how to use instructional strategies that promote student learning.

The teacher understands that students' physical, social, emotional, moral, and cognitive development influence learning and knows how to address these factors when making instructional decisions.

The teacher is aware of expected developmental progressions and the ranges of individual variation within each domain (physical, social, emotional, moral, and cognitive), can identify levels of readiness in learning, and understands how development in any one domain may affect performance in others.

Dispositions

The teacher appreciates individual variations within each area of development, shows respect for the diverse talents of all learners, and is committed to help them develop self-confidence and competence.

The teacher is disposed to use students' strengths as a basis for growth, and their errors as an opportunity for learning.

Shaded means that the standard is not covered in the *Principles of Learning and Teaching* tests.

Principles of Learning and Teaching Test Topics

INTASC Standards

Student development and the learning process	Principle 2: The teacher understands how children learn and develop, and can provide learning opportunities that support their intellectual, social and personal development.
When responding to case studies, you will be asked to perform the following kinds of tasks related to the area of human development and the learning process: Identify and describe strengths and/or weaknesses in — the instruction described in the case, in terms of its appropriateness for students at a particular age Propose a strategy for — instruction that would appropriate for students at the age described in the case — incorporating activities that will have students described in the case draw on their own experiences to understand the instruction — stimulating prior knowledge in the situation described in the case	**Performances** The teacher assesses individual and group performance in order to design instruction that meets learners' current needs in each domain (cognitive, social, emotional, moral, and physical) and that leads to the next level of development. The teacher stimulates student reflection on prior knowledge and links new ideas to already familiar ideas, making connections to students' experiences, providing opportunities for active engagement, manipulation, and testing of ideas and materials, and encouraging students to assume responsibility for shaping their learning tasks. The teacher accesses students' thinking and experiences as a basis for instructional activities by, for example, encouraging discussion, listening and responding to group interaction, and eliciting samples of student thinking orally and in writing.

Shaded means that the standard is not covered in the *Principles of Learning and Teaching* tests.

Principles of Learning and Teaching Test Topics

INTASC Standards

Students as diverse learners	Principle 3: The teacher understands how students differ in their approaches to learning and creates instructional opportunities that are adapted to diverse learners.
	Knowledge
Differences in the ways students learn and perform ▪ Learning styles, multiple intelligences, performance modes, gender differences, cultural expectations and styles	The teacher understands and can identify differences in approaches to learning and performance, including different learning styles, multiple intelligences, and performance modes, and can design instruction that helps use students' strengths as the basis for growth.
Areas of exceptionality in students' learning ▪ Major types of challenges in each category, major symptoms, major classroom and instructional issues related to each area	The teacher knows about areas of exceptionality in learning—including learning disabilities, visual and perceptual difficulties, and special physical or mental challenges.
Legislation and institutional responsibilities relating to exceptional students	
The process of second language acquisition and strategies to support the learning of students for whom English is not a first language	The teacher knows about the process of second language acquisition and about strategies to support the learning of students whose first language is not English.
How students' learning is influenced by individual experiences, talents, and prior learning, as well as language, culture, family, and community values	The teacher understands how students' learning is influenced by individual experiences, talents, and prior learning, as well as language, culture, family, and community values.

Shaded means that the standard is not covered in the *Principles of Learning and Teaching* tests.

Principles of Learning and Teaching Test Topics

INTASC Standards

Students as diverse learners	Principle 3: The teacher understands how students differ in their approaches to learning and creates instructional opportunities that are adapted to diverse learners.
	The teacher has a well-grounded framework for understanding cultural and community diversity and knows how to learn about and incorporate students' experiences, cultures, and community resources into instruction.
	Dispositions
	The teacher believes that all children can learn at high levels and persists in helping all children achieve success.
	The teacher appreciates and values human diversity, shows respect for students' varied talents and perspectives, and is committed to the pursuit of "individually configured excellence."
	The teacher respects students as individuals with differing personal and family backgrounds and various skills, talents, and interests.
	The teacher is sensitive to community and cultural norms.
	The teacher makes students feel valued for their potential as people, and helps them learn to value each other.

Shaded means that the standard is not covered in the *Principles of Learning and Teaching* tests.

Principles of Learning and Teaching Test Topics	INTASC *Standards*
Students as diverse learners	**Principle 3: The teacher understands how students differ in their approaches to learning and creates instructional opportunities that are adapted to diverse learners.**
▶ Approaches for accommodating various learning styles, intelligences, or exceptionalities ▶ When responding to case studies, you will be asked to perform the following kinds of tasks related to the area of students as diverse learners: Identify and describe a strength and/or weakness in — a lesson plan for meeting needs of individual students with identified special needs, as described in the case — the interaction described in the case between the teacher and students in terms of culturally responsive teaching	**Performances** The teacher identifies and designs instruction appropriate to students' stages of development, learning styles, strengths, and needs. The teacher uses teaching approaches that are sensitive to the multiple experiences of learners and that address different learning and performance modes. The teacher makes appropriate provisions (in terms of time and circumstances for work, tasks assigned, communication and response modes) for individual students who have particular learning differences or needs. The teacher can identify when and how to access appropriate services or resources to meet exceptional learning needs. The teacher seeks to understand students' families, cultures, and communities, and uses this information as a basis for connecting instruction to students' experiences. The teacher brings multiple perspectives to the discussion of subject matter, including attention to students' personal, family, and community experiences and cultural norms. The teacher creates a learning community in which individual differences are respected.

Shaded means that the standard is not covered in the *Principles of Learning and Teaching* tests.

Principles of Learning and Teaching Test Topics

INTASC *Standards*

Students as diverse learners	Principle 3: The teacher understands how students differ in their approaches to learning and creates instructional opportunities that are adapted to diverse learners.
Propose a strategy for — helping students with attention deficit problems described in the case stay on task (e.g., in listening to a lecture, following a demonstration, doing written work) — improving performance of students in the case who do not perform well on homework, original compositions, or other assignments — helping students in the case for whom English is not the first language build literacy skills and/or improve in academic areas — meeting the needs of a wide range of students (especially students with learning difficulties and students who are accelerated) — building positive relationships with a student the case shows is very turned off to school — adapting instruction and/or assessment for an individual student with identified needs described in the case — helping the students described in the case see issues from different points of view	

Shaded means that the standard is not covered in the *Principles of Learning and Teaching* tests.

Principles of Learning and Teaching Test Topics

INTASC Standards

Instructional strategies	Principle 4: The teacher understands and uses a variety of instructional strategies to encourage students' development of critical thinking, problem solving, and performance skills.
	Knowledge
▸ The major cognitive processes associated with student learning	The teacher understands the cognitive processes associated with various kinds of learning and how these processes can be stimulated.
▸ Major categories, advantages, and appropriate uses of instructional strategies	The teacher understands principles and techniques associated with various instructional strategies.
▸ Methods for enhancing student learning through the use of a variety of resources and materials	The teacher knows how to enhance student learning through the use of a variety of resources and materials as well as human and technological resources.
	Dispositions The teacher values the development of students' critical thinking, independent problem solving, and performance capabilities. The teacher values flexibility and reciprocity in the teaching process as necessary for adapting instruction to student responses, ideas, and needs.
▸ Principles, techniques, and methods associated with major instructional strategies, especially direct instruction and student-centered models	**Performances** The teacher carefully evaluates how to achieve learning goals, choosing alternative teaching strategies and materials to achieve instructional purposes and to meet students' needs.

Shaded means that the standard is not covered in the *Principles of Learning and Teaching* tests.

Principles of Learning and Teaching Test Topics

INTASC Standards

Instructional strategies	Principle 4: The teacher understands and uses a variety of instructional strategies to encourage students' development of critical thinking, problem solving, and performance skills.
When responding to case studies, you will be asked to perform the following kinds of tasks related to the area of instructional planning: Identify and describe a strength and/or weakness in — specific activities that are described in the case Propose a strategy for — teaching critical thinking skills in a specific lesson described in the case — achieving effectiveness with group work in a particular situation described in the case — helping students stay on task in the situation described in the case — helping students learn material presented through various media introduced in the case — assigning students to group work, appropriate to the case — bringing closure to a lesson that stops abruptly in the case — improving student interaction during class discussion as described in the case — addressing a "missed opportunity" during instruction that is described in the case	The teacher uses multiple teaching and learning strategies to engage students in active learning opportunities that promote the development of critical thinking, problem solving, and performance capabilities and that help students assume responsibility for identifying and using learning resources. The teacher constantly monitors and adjusts strategies in response to student feedback. The teacher varies his or her roles (e.g. instructor, facilitator, coach, audience) in relation to the content and purposes of instruction and the needs of students. The teacher develops a variety of clear, accurate presentations and representations of concepts, using alternative explanations to assist students' understanding and presenting diverse perspectives to encourage critical thinking.

Shaded means that the standard is not covered in the *Principles of Learning and Teaching* tests.

Principles of Learning and Teaching Test Topics

INTASC *Standards*

Student motivation and the learning environment	Principle 5: The teacher uses an understanding of individual and group motivation and behavior to create a learning environment that encourages positive social interaction, active engagement in learning, and self-motivation.
Theoretical foundations about human motivation and behavior ■ Important theorists and theories ■ Important concepts and terms **How knowledge of human motivation and behavior should influence strategies for organizing and supporting individual and group work in the classroom** **Factors and situations that are likely to promote or diminish students' motivation to learn; how to help students become self-motivated**	**Knowledge** The teacher can use knowledge about human motivation and behavior drawn from the foundational sciences of psychology, anthropology, and sociology to develop strategies for organizing and supporting individual and group work. The teacher understands how social groups function and influence people, and how people influence groups. The teacher knows how to help people work productively and cooperatively with each other in complex social settings. The teacher recognizes factors and situations that are likely to promote or diminish intrinsic motivation, and knows how to help students become self-motivated.

Shaded means that the standard is not covered in the *Principles of Learning and Teaching* tests.

Principles of Learning and Teaching Test Topics	INTASC *Standards*
Student motivation and the learning environment	**Principle 5: The teacher uses an understanding of individual and group motivation and behavior to create a learning environment that encourages positive social interaction, active engagement in learning, and self-motivation.**
	Dispositions The teacher takes responsibility for establishing a positive climate in the classroom and participates in maintaining such a climate in the school as a whole. The teacher understands how participation supports commitment, and is committed to the expression and use of democratic values in the classroom. The teacher values the role of students in promoting each other's learning and recognizes the importance of peer relationships in establishing a climate of learning. The teacher recognizes the value of intrinsic motivation to students' life-long growth and learning. The teacher is committed to continuous development of individual students' abilities and considers how different motivational strategies are likely to encourage this development for each student.

Shaded means that the standard is not covered in the *Principles of Learning and Teaching* tests.

Principles of Learning and Teaching Test Topics

INTASC *Standards*

Principles of Learning and Teaching Test Topics	INTASC Standards
Student motivation and the learning environment	**Principle 5: The teacher uses an understanding of individual and group motivation and behavior to create a learning environment that encourages positive social interaction, active engagement in learning, and self-motivation.**
▶ Principles of effective classroom management and strategies to promote positive relationships, cooperation, and purposeful learning	**Performances**

The teacher creates a smoothly functioning learning community in which students assume responsibility for themselves and one another, participate in decision-making, work collaboratively and independently, and engage in purposeful learning activities.

The teacher engages students in individual and cooperative learning activities that help them develop the motivation to achieve.

The teacher organizes, allocates, and manages the resources of time, space, activities, and attention to provide active and equitable engagement of students in productive tasks.

The teacher maximizes the amount of class time spent in learning by creating expectations and processes for communication and behavior, along with a physical setting conducive to classroom goals. |

Shaded means that the standard is not covered in the *Principles of Learning and Teaching* tests.

Principles of Learning and Teaching Test Topics

INTASC Standards

Student motivation and the learning environment	Principle 5: The teacher uses an understanding of individual and group motivation and behavior to create a learning environment that encourages positive social interaction, active engagement in learning, and self-motivation.

▶ When responding to case studies, you will be asked to perform the following kinds of tasks related to the area of student motivation and the learning environment:
 	
    Identify and describe a strength and/or weakness in
 	
    — a lesson plan or instructional strategy described in the case with the intention of building a positive classroom environment
 	
    Propose a strategy for
 	
    — revising a lesson that is described in the case for improving student engagement and motivation
 	
    — improving motivation through means other than negative strategies described in the case
 	
    — addressing behavioral problems that are described in the case
	The teacher helps the group to develop shared values and expectations for student interactions, academic discussions, and individual and group responsibility that create a positive classroom climate of openness, mutual respect, support, and inquiry.
	
	The teacher analyzes the classroom environment and makes decisions and adjustments to enhance social relationships, student motivation and engagement, and productive work.
	
	The teacher organizes, prepares students for, and monitors independent and group work that allows for full and varied participation of all individuals.

Shaded means that the standard is not covered in the *Principles of Learning and Teaching* tests.

Principles of Learning and Teaching Test Topics

INTASC *Standards*

Communication techniques	**Principle 6: The teacher uses knowledge of effective verbal, nonverbal, and media communication techniques to foster active inquiry, collaboration, and supportive interaction in the classroom.**
▶ Basic, effective verbal and nonverbal communication techniques ▶ The effect of cultural and gender differences on communications in the classroom	**Knowledge** The teacher understands communication theory, language development, and the role of language in learning. The teacher understands how cultural and gender differences can affect communications in the classroom. The teacher recognizes the importance of nonverbal as well as verbal communication. The teacher knows about and can use effective verbal, nonverbal, and media communication techniques.

Shaded means that the standard is not covered in the *Principles of Learning and Teaching* tests.

Principles of Learning and Teaching Test Topics

INTASC Standards

Communication techniques	Principle 6: The teacher uses knowledge of effective verbal, nonverbal, and media communication techniques to foster active inquiry, collaboration, and supportive interaction in the classroom.
	Dispositions The teacher recognizes the power of language for fostering self-expression, identity development, and learning. The teacher values many ways in which people seek to communicate and encourages many modes of communication in the classroom. The teacher is a thoughtful and responsive listener. The teacher appreciates the cultural dimensions of communication, responds appropriately, and seeks to foster culturally sensitive communication by and among all students in the class.

Shaded means that the standard is not covered in the *Principles of Learning and Teaching* tests.

Principles of Learning and Teaching Test Topics

INTASC Standards

Communication techniques	Principle 6: The teacher uses knowledge of effective verbal, nonverbal, and media communication techniques to foster active inquiry, collaboration, and supportive interaction in the classroom.

▸ Types of questions that can stimulate discussion in different ways for particular purposes
 	
▸ When responding to case studies, you will be asked to perform the following kinds of tasks related to the area of communication:
 	
  Identify and describe a strength and/or weakness in
 	
  — the teacher's oral or written communication with students in the case (e.g., feedback on assignments, interaction during class)
 	
  Propose a strategy for
 	
  — improving the self-image of a student described in the case or the student's sense of responsibility for his or her own learning
 	
  — involving all students in a class discussion described in the case in a positive way, showing respect for others
 	
  — helping a student described in the case to develop social skills in a specified situation
	Performances
	
	The teacher models effective communication strategies in conveying ideas and information and in asking questions.
	
	The teacher supports and expands learner expression in speaking, writing, and other media.
	
	The teacher knows how to ask questions and stimulate discussion in different ways for particular purposes.
	
	The teacher communicates in ways that demonstrate a sensitivity to cultural and gender differences.
	
	The teacher knows how to use a variety of media communication tools, including audio-visual aids and computers, to enrich students' learning opportunities.

Shaded means that the standard is not covered in the *Principles of Learning and Teaching* tests.

Principles of Learning and Teaching Test Topics

INTASC Standards

Planning instruction	Principle 7: The teacher plans instruction based upon knowledge of subject matter, students, the community, and curriculum goals.
▶ Techniques for planning instruction to meet curriculum goals, including the incorporation of learning theory, subject matter, curriculum development, and student development ▶ Techniques for creating effective bridges between curriculum goals and students' experiences	**Knowledge** The teacher understands learning theory, subject matter, curriculum development, and student development and knows how to use this knowledge in planning instruction to meet curriculum goals. The teacher knows how to take contextual considerations (instructional materials, individual student interests, needs, and aptitudes, and community resources) into account in planning instruction that creates an effective bridge between curriculum goals and students' experiences. The teacher knows when and how to adjust plans based on student responses and other contingencies. **Dispositions** The teacher values both long term and short term planning. The teacher believes that plans must always be open to adjustment and revision based on student needs and changing circumstances. The teacher values planning as a collegial activity.

Shaded means that the standard is not covered in the *Principles of Learning and Teaching* tests.

Principles of Learning and Teaching Test Topics

INTASC *Standards*

Planning instruction	Principle 7: The teacher plans instruction based upon knowledge of subject matter, students, the community, and curriculum goals.

Performances

When responding to case studies, you will be asked to perform the following kinds of tasks related to the area of instructional planning:

As an individual and a member of a team, the teacher selects and creates learning experiences that are appropriate for curriculum goals, relevant to learners, and based upon principles of effective instruction.

Identify and describe a strength and/or weakness in

— a unit plan that is described in the case

— specific strategies used in instruction (e.g., using lecture, using class discussion) in the case

— a sequence of lessons described in the case designed to achieve a goal or set of objectives

— one or more written assignments given to students in the case

Propose a strategy for

— meeting what may appear to be conflicting goals or objectives described in the case

— teaching specific kinds of skills (e.g., improving writing fluency, vocabulary)

The teacher plans for learning opportunities that recognize and address variation in learning styles and performance modes.

The teacher creates lessons and activities that operate at multiple levels to meet the developmental and individual needs of diverse learners and help each progress.

The teacher creates short-range and long-term plans that are linked to student needs and performance and adapts the plans to ensure and capitalize on student progress and motivation.

The teacher responds to unanticipated sources of input, evaluates plans in relation to short- and long-range goals, and systematically adjusts plans to meet student needs and enhance learning.

Shaded means that the standard is not covered in the *Principles of Learning and Teaching* tests.

Principles of Learning and Teaching Test Topics

INTASC *Standards*

Assessment strategies	Principle 8: The teacher understands and uses formal and informal assessment strategies to evaluate and ensure the continuous intellectual, social, and physical development of the learner.
▶ Types of assessments ▶ Characteristics of assessments ▶ Scoring assessments ▶ Uses of assessments ▶ Measurement theory and assessment-related issues ▶ Interpreting and communicating results of assessments	**Knowledge** The teacher understands the characteristics, uses, advantages, and limitations of different types of assessments for evaluating how students learn, what they know and are able to do, and what kinds of experiences will support their further growth and development. The teacher knows how to select, construct, and use assessment strategies and instruments appropriate to the learning outcomes being evaluated and to other diagnostic purposes. The teacher understands measurement theory and assessment-related issues such as validity, reliability, bias, and scoring concerns. **Dispositions** The teacher values ongoing assessment as essential to the instructional process and recognizes that many different assessment strategies, accurately and systematically used, are necessary for monitoring and promoting student learning. The teacher is committed to using assessment to identify student strengths and promote student growth rather than to deny students access to learning opportunities.

Shaded means that the standard is not covered in the *Principles of Learning and Teaching* tests.

Principles of Learning and Teaching Test Topics

INTASC Standards

Assessment strategies	Principle 8: The teacher understands and uses formal and informal assessment strategies to evaluate and ensure the continuous intellectual, social, and physical development of the learner.

Performances

When responding to case studies, you will be asked to perform the following kinds of tasks related to the area of assessment:

Propose a strategy for

— assessing progress of students described in the case toward specified goals or objectives

— assessing class progress toward achievement of specified goals or objectives

— gathering information to use to help understand class performance that is different from what was expected at the beginning of the year

— assessing language fluency of a student in a case for whom English is not the first language

Propose a hypothesis or explanation for

— a student's strengths and/or weaknesses as a learner based on the evidence presented

— what might be important to explore in working with a student described in the case who is having difficulties academically, socially, or emotionally

The teacher appropriately uses a variety of formal and informal assessment techniques to enhance her or his knowledge of learners, evaluate students' progress and performances, and modify teaching and learning strategies.

The teacher solicits and uses information about students' experiences, learning behavior, needs, and progress from parents, other colleagues, and the students themselves.

The teacher uses assessment strategies to involve learners in self-assessment activities, to help them become aware of their strengths and needs, and to encourage them to set personal goals for learning.

The teacher evaluates the effect of class activities on both individual students and the class as a whole, collecting information through observation of classroom interactions, questioning, and analysis of student work.

Shaded means that the standard is not covered in the *Principles of Learning and Teaching* tests.

Principles of Learning and Teaching Test Topics

INTASC *Standards*

Assessment strategies	**Principle 8: The teacher understands and uses formal and informal assessment strategies to evaluate and ensure the continuous intellectual, social, and physical development of the learner.**
	The teacher monitors his or her own teaching strategies and behavior in relation to student success, modifying plans and instructional approaches accordingly. The teacher maintains useful records of student work and can communicate student progress knowledgeably and responsibly, based on appropriate indicators, to students, parents, and other colleagues.

Shaded means that the standard is not covered in the *Principles of Learning and Teaching* tests.

Principles of Learning and Teaching Test Topics

INTASC Standards

The reflective practitioner	Principle 9: The teacher is a reflective practitioner who continually evaluates the effects of his/her choices and actions on others (students, parents, and other professionals in the learning community) and who actively seeks out opportunities to grow professionally.
▸ Why personal reflection on teaching practices is critical, and approaches that can be used to do so	**Knowledge** The teacher understands methods of inquiry that provide him/her with a variety of self-assessment and problem-solving strategies for reflecting on his/her practice, its influences on students' growth and learning, and the complex interactions between them.
▸ Ability to read and understand articles and books about current views, ideas, and debates regarding best teaching practices ▸ Types of resources available for professional development and learning	The teacher is aware of major areas of research on teaching and of resources available for professional learning (e.g. professional literature, colleagues, professional associations, professional development activities).
	Dispositions The teacher values critical thinking and self-directed learning as habits of mind. The teacher is committed to reflection, assessment, and learning as an ongoing process. The teacher is willing to give and receive help. The teacher is committed to seeking out, developing, and continually refining practices that address the individual needs of students.

Shaded means that the standard is not covered in the *Principles of Learning and Teaching* tests.

Principles of Learning and Teaching Test Topics

INTASC *Standards*

The reflective practitioner	Principle 9: The teacher is a reflective practitioner who continually evaluates the effects of his/her choices and actions on others (students, parents, and other professionals in the learning community) and who actively seeks out opportunities to grow professionally.
	The teacher recognizes his/her professional responsibility for engaging in and supporting appropriate professional practices for self and colleagues. **Performances** The teacher uses classroom observation, information about students, and research as sources for evaluating the outcomes of teaching and learning and as a basis for experimenting with, reflecting on, and revising practice. The teacher seeks out professional literature, colleagues, and other resources to support his/her own development as a learner and a teacher. The teacher draws upon professional colleagues within the school and other professional arenas as supports for reflection, problem-solving and new ideas, actively sharing experiences, and seeking and giving feedback.

Shaded means that the standard is not covered in the *Principles of Learning and Teaching* tests.

Principles of Learning and Teaching Test Topics

INTASC *Standards*

The larger community	**Principle 10: The teacher fosters relationships with school colleagues, parents, and agencies in the larger community to support students' learning and well-being.**
	Knowledge
▸ The role of the school as a resource to the larger community	The teacher understands schools as organizations within the larger community context and understands the operations of the relevant aspects of the system(s) within which s/he works.
▸ Factors in the students' environment outside of school (family circumstances, community environments, health and economic conditions) that may influence students' life and learning	The teacher understands how factors in the students' environment outside of school may influence students' life and learning.
▸ Basic strategies for involving parents/ guardians and leaders in the community in the educational process	
▸ Major laws related to students' rights and teacher responsibilities	The teacher understands and implements laws related to students' rights and teacher responsibilities.

Shaded means that the standard is not covered in the *Principles of Learning and Teaching* tests.

Principles of Learning and Teaching Test Topics

INTASC *Standards*

The larger community	**Principle 10: The teacher fosters relationships with school colleagues, parents, and agencies in the larger community to support students' learning and well-being.**
	Dispositions The teacher values and appreciates the importance of all aspects of a child's experience. The teacher is concerned about all aspects of a child's well-being, and is alert to signs of difficulties. The teacher is willing to consult with other adults regarding the education and well-being of his/her students. The teacher respects the privacy of students and confidentiality of information. The teacher is willing to work with other professionals to improve the overall learning environment for students.

Shaded means that the standard is not covered in the *Principles of Learning and Teaching* tests.

Principles of Learning and Teaching Test Topics

INTASC Standards

The larger community	Principle 10: The teacher fosters relationships with school colleagues, parents, and agencies in the larger community to support students' learning and well-being

Performances

▶ When responding to case studies, you will be asked to perform the following kinds of tasks related to the area of the larger community:

Identify and describe a strength and/or weakness in

— the communication with parents used by a teacher described in the case

— the approach used by a teacher as described in the case to involve parents

Propose a strategy for

— using parent volunteers during a lesson that is described in a case

— involving all parents or other caregivers in helping students in areas specified in the case

— helping the family of a student described in the case work with the student's learning or other needs

The teacher participates in collegial activities designed to make the entire school a productive learning environment.

The teacher makes links with the learners' other environments on behalf of students by consulting with parents, counselors, teachers of other classes and activities within the schools, and professionals in other community agencies.

The teacher can identify and use community resources to foster student learning.

The teacher establishes respectful and productive relationships with parents and guardians from diverse home and community situations, and seeks to develop cooperative partnerships in support of student learning and well-being.

The teacher talks with and listens to the student, is sensitive and responsive to clues of distress, investigates situations, and seeks outside help as needed and appropriate to remedy problems.

The teacher acts as an advocate for students.

Shaded means that the standard is not covered in the *Principles of Learning and Teaching* tests.

Chapter 4

How to Read a Case Study

▶ ▶ ▶ ▶ ▶ ▶ ▶ ▶ ▶ ▶ ▶ ▶

How to Read a Case Study

Why case studies are used on this test

ETS uses case studies as the basis for this assessment of a beginning teacher's professional and pedagogical knowledge for several important reasons.

- First, professional educators frequently use case studies of teaching situations as a method for representing the complex domain of professional practice. Carefully constructed, case studies can simulate actual teaching contexts, issues, and challenges. They also provide a platform for thinking about theoretical and practical pedagogical concerns, making them a professionally credible method for assessing an educator's knowledge.

- Second, case studies allow the presentation of sufficient detail about a particular teaching situation or series of classroom events. By identifying strengths and weaknesses in the teaching presented, case studies provide a medium in which hypotheses, conclusions, and suggestions for strategies that might accomplish particular pedagogical goals can be thoughtfully supported and explained.

- Third, case studies encourage questions that demand application of knowledge across a broad range of professional knowledge bases—developmental psychology, motivation, communication strategies, pedagogical methods and strategies, instructional design principles and strategies—rather than simple recognition and recall of facts without a meaningful context.

Simulations of teaching situations like those presented in the *Principles of Learning and Teaching* case studies offer the opportunity to ask questions that may have several acceptable answers. The open-ended questions that follow each case study encourage the beginning teacher to synthesize knowledge much as he or she will have to in the day-to-day work of teaching. Because the open-ended questions can be satisfactorily answered from multiple different perspectives, they acknowledge that teachers have extremely varied backgrounds and experiences with students, and that there are often many possible effective responses in a given teaching situation.

Two kinds of cases: teacher-based and student-based

You may encounter either or both of two kinds of cases in the *Principles of Learning and Teaching* test. The first is a "teacher-based" case and the second is a "student-based" case. The first type focuses on the teaching practice of one or more teachers. The case will present sufficient information about the teaching context, goals, objectives, lesson plans, assignments, teaching strategies, assessments, and interactions with students to enable you to identify the issues involved in the case and to respond fully to the questions about the teachers' practices. However, the information is carefully restricted to only what is required to understand the issues and respond to the questions; additional information might be interesting to have but is not essential for understanding and responding. A response that says the question cannot be answered because more information is needed is not acceptable; all information required to respond is presented in the case.

The second type of case is "student-based." This focuses on one student, with information about the student's background, where appropriate, and the student's strengths and weaknesses. In addition, there may be examples of the student's work as well as excerpts of conversations between the student and a teacher, counselor, or interviewer. Excerpts of a class discussion in which the student participated may also be provided. Again, the information provided is what you need to understand the issues involved and to respond to the questions. As with teacher-based cases, you might want to know more about the student, but all the information you need to respond fully to each question is presented.

Although cases are termed "student-based" and "teacher-based," both kinds of cases often have questions that deal with both teachers and students as learners. For example, one of the cases presented below is termed a student-based case because one student is the focus of the case. However, the teacher's practice is clearly an essential part of the case, and there are questions that focus both on the student as a learner and on the teacher's practice.

All case studies are approximately the same length, 800–850 words, and each is followed by three questions requiring a "constructed response." This means that for each question, you need to write one or two paragraphs to answer the question. In no case are there questions that require knowledge specific to academic disciplines such as language arts, history, science, or mathematics.

Two different formats, narrative and document-based

Both kinds of cases, teacher-based and student-based, may be presented in either of two formats. The first format is narrative and the second is document-based. A narrative case presents an objective account of what happens within an educational setting—a classroom, set of classrooms, or a school as a whole. The case does not present "the whole story" about the teacher or student, but rather a focused account of certain issues, with the information necessary to respond fully to the questions. For example, in a student-based case, the narrative does not tell what other students in the classroom are doing unless their actions are relevant to understanding the central student. If the focus is on a teacher, the narrative is restricted to that part of the teacher's activities and responsibilities directly related to the case and the questions.

The second format is document-based. The case consists of a set of three or more documents that relate to the teacher or student on whom the case is focused. Teacher-based cases might include such documents as lesson or short unit plans, assignments, student work, notes from observations by mentors or supervisors, notes from parents or counselors, assessments, and teacher journals. Student-based cases might include such documents as excerpts from student records; excerpts from conversations between the student and a teacher, counselor or another staff member; examples of student work; notes from parents or counselors; and excerpts from class or small group discussions.

How should you read a case study?

Two expert strategies

You may want to use one or both of the two expert strategies presented here for reading case studies. The key to both of them is a close and careful reading of the case, with attention focused on the important information in *each* paragraph or document. You will also want to consider how each paragraph or document relates to the central issues addressed in the case and in the questions.

The first strategy is to read the case study with the major content categories (presented in chapter 3) clearly in mind. Remember that each case and the questions are based directly on these categories. You will also want to keep in mind that each paragraph of the narrative or each document is included specifically to elicit understanding of an issue or to provide information for responding to the questions.

Therefore, for each section, narrative, or document, ask the following questions as you read:

- What issues about the teacher's planning, instruction, and assessment does this raise?

- What issues are raised about the student as a learner and the way teachers and others do and/or do not understand and address the student's strengths and needs?

- What specific information is presented here that addresses the way issues were faced and resolved? How else might they have been resolved?

- How, specifically, does this information address one or more of the questions?

The second strategy is to read the questions that follow the case first—*before* you read the case. Once you have carefully examined the questions and made mental notes about what kinds of issues to look for in the case, then you can then read the case and take notes about how each paragraph, section, and/or document relates to particular questions.

Reading a case with content categories in mind

To help you understand more about what case studies look like and how the first expert approach might work for you, a sample case with annotations is presented on the following page. This narrative, about Sara, is a student-based case that involves issues about Sara as a learner and about Ms. Mercer, her first-grade teacher. Follow the case and note the questions raised in the marginal notes. These questions relate to the major content categories covered on the test.

SARA

Scenario

Six-year-old Sara lives with her mother, who has a relaxed schedule. Ms. Mercer, Sara's teacher, notes that Sara is often tired and inattentive after arriving late. Sara says she frequently stays up past midnight if others are up. Ms. Mercer, a second-year teacher, has asked her mentor to observe Sara and suggest ways to help Sara achieve Ms. Mercer's purposes.

Observation: Ms. Mercer's Class, April 30

Pre-observation interview notes

Ms. Mercer says, "The purposes of first grade are to teach children 'school survival skills' and reading, writing, and arithmetic." She adds, "Sara needs help with 'survival skills,' including following directions, concentrating on a task to its completion, and being attentive to the lessons I present."

Mentor classroom observation—focus on Sara Porter

As Ms. Mercer's class begins, the children play with puzzles and other activities requiring construction or manipulation. Two children "write" on a flannel board, using letters kept in alphabetical stacks in a box. They return the letters so they fit exactly over their counterparts. Ms. Mercer praises them for neatness. She instructs them to return to their previously assigned groups as Sara enters the room.

The students are seated at six tables, four students at each table. Ms. Mercer explains, "Tables one and two will work on reading first, while tables three and four will solve math problems, and tables five and six will draw page illustrations for your collaborative Big Book. After twenty-five minutes, the groups will stop the first activity and begin working on a second task without changing seats. Twenty-five minutes later, you will change again to work on the activity each group has not yet done. The math

Sidebar questions

What possible issues does this section suggest about Sara as a learner? How might this information be useful in thinking about these issues?

What possible issues are raised about Ms. Mercer's approach to teaching first grade? How might these affect Sara?

What does this section tell us about Ms. Mercer's approach and how it might impact Sara?

What issues about Ms. Mercer's approach does this section raise? What strengths and/or areas for improvement in her use of group work might this suggest?

groups and those doing illustrations will hand in their work when time is called. I will work with the two groups who are reading aloud." She plans to monitor progress of students in the reading group.

Sara is at table one. Ms. Mercer begins with this table and table two, working on reading. Several children read aloud. Ms. Mercer praises them. When Ms. Mercer calls on Sara, she begins reading in the wrong place. Joyce, seated next to Sara, points to where they are. Ms. Mercer says, "Sara, you would know where we are if you were paying attention." She calls on another child. Sara looks hurt, but soon starts to follow along in the book. Subsequently, Ms. Mercer calls on Sara, who now has the right place. Ms. Mercer then calls on another child.

> What information does this section present about Sara as a learner? How might this information be used?

During the math activity, Sara, yawning frequently, is the last to open her workbook and write her name. When she completes the page, she waits. She seems puzzled, although Ms. Mercer has already given directions. Sara gets up, sharpens a pencil, and returns to the wrong seat. "That's MY seat," accuses an angry boy. Sara apologizes and returns to her seat. Later, she waits to have her workbook checked. She has not torn out pages as Ms. Mercer instructed. Sara is told to "do it right." Sara has not creased the paper as Ms. Mercer demonstrated, so the pages do not tear out easily. Sara sucks her thumb and holds her ear for a minute. Suddenly, she yanks the paper and the pages come out with jagged edges. She receives three dots for her work. Ms. Mercer says, "Sara, this is good. I wish you could earn four dots" (the maximum). Sara slaps herself on the forehead.

> What additional information about Sara as a learner is presented? What issues might this information raise? How does Ms. Mercer interact with Sara? How might this be important?

During the illustration activity, Sara helps several others who have trouble thinking of ideas. Sara's illustration is among the best handed in.

What additional information about Sara is presented? How might this be important in addressing her strengths and needs? How might the information about Ms. Mercer's writing lesson be important? What strengths or areas for improvement might it suggest? How might it be built upon?

What are the implications of the mentor's comment?

After the group work, Ms. Mercer places a large pad on an easel and says, "Now we're going to write about our trip to the art museum yesterday. Raise your hand and tell me something you saw or did in the museum." No one responds. She says, "Tell me the first thing we did at the museum." Sara raises her hand, offering a first sentence. After each response, Ms. Mercer asks, "What happened next?" or "What did we see next?" She prints each child's contribution.

Our Trip to the Art Museum

We rode the elevator to the second floor. We looked at different shapes on the ceiling. We saw a statue with a white triangle. We went to another room where we saw some pictures. We rode back down to the first floor. On our way out, we saw a painting of a grandfather and a boy.

During the writing of the group story, Sara fidgets in her seat, stares out the window, and makes a face at her neighbor.

Post-observation interview notes

Ms. Mercer says, "Sara is a top performer in academic achievement and on standardized tests, consistently scoring among the top five students in the class. She's so bright. It's a shame she's late and distracted so much." The mentor replies, "There may be something else bothering Sara. Although she is easily distracted, there may be other explanations for her behavior. Let's talk more."

Reading a case with the questions in mind

The same case will be presented again, but this time using the second expert method. First read through the questions below, then read through the case again with question-related notes. Notice that these notes next to the case show how each paragraph or section relates to a particular question, and propose some ideas that will eventually go into the actual response to the questions.

Questions related to the case about Sara

1. Suppose that Ms. Mercer and her mentor discuss how to connect school and Sara's home environment for the benefit of Sara's learning.

    ▪ Identify TWO specific actions Ms. Mercer might take to connect school and Sara's home environment for the benefit of Sara's learning.

    ▪ Explain how each action you identified could benefit Sara's learning. Base your response on principles of fostering school-parent relationships to support student learning.

2. Review the pre-observation notes in which Ms. Mercer explains the purposes of first grade as she sees them. Suppose that her mentor suggests that Ms. Mercer consider other purposes of first grade and how she might modify her instruction to address those purposes and the related needs of Sara and her other students.

    ▪ Identify TWO additional purposes of first grade that Ms. Mercer could consider when planning her instruction, in order to meet the needs of Sara and/or her other students.

    ▪ For each purpose you identified, explain how Ms. Mercer might modify her instruction to address the purpose and meet the needs of Sara and/or her other students. Base your response on principles of planning instruction and learning theory.

3. Assume that the groups working on mathematics and illustrations for the Big Book become very noisy and unproductive over the course of the activity.

    ▪ Suggest TWO changes Ms. Mercer could have made in the planning and/or implementation of the group work that would have made the activity more successful.

    ▪ Explain how each suggested change you suggested could have made the group work activity more successful. Base your response on principles of planning instruction and human development.

4. In the activities described in the Mentor Classroom Observation, Ms. Mercer demonstrates understanding of developmentally appropriate instruction.

    ▪ Identify TWO strengths in the instructional approaches Ms. Mercer uses in the activities that reflect understanding of the principles of developmentally appropriate instruction.

    ▪ Explain how each of these strengths you identified provides evidence of an understanding of the principles of developmentally appropriate instruction. Base your response on principles of planning instruction and human development.

5. Assume that the day after the lesson was observed, Ms. Mercer's objective is to use the story about the museum visit to continue building students' literacy.

- Identify TWO strategies and/or activities involving the story about the museum visit that Ms. Mercer could use to continue building students' literacy.

- For each strategy and/or activity you identified, explain how it could help build literacy. Base your response on principles of language development and acquisition.

6. In the post-observation notes, Ms. Mercer's mentor suggests that they explore explanations for Sara's inattentive behavior.

- Suggest TWO hypotheses other than lack of sleep that Ms. Mercer and her mentor might explore to learn more about why Sara behaves as she does in class.

- For each hypothesis you suggested, describe at least one action that Ms. Mercer and her mentor might take to see if the hypothesis might be correct. Base your response on principles of human development, motivation, and diagnostic assessment.

SARA

Scenario

Six-year-old Sara lives with her mother, who has a relaxed schedule. Ms. Mercer, Sara's teacher, notes that Sara is often tired and inattentive after arriving late. Sara says she frequently stays up past midnight if others are up. Ms. Mercer, a second-year teacher, has asked her mentor to observe Sara and suggest ways to help Sara achieve Ms. Mercer's purposes.

Observation: Ms. Mercer's Class, April 30

Pre-observation interview notes

Ms. Mercer says, "The purposes of first grade are to teach children 'school survival skills' and reading, writing, and arithmetic." She adds, "Sara needs help with 'survival skills,' including following directions, concentrating on a task to its completion, and being attentive to the lessons I present."

Mentor classroom observation—focus on Sara Porter

As Ms. Mercer's class begins, the children play with puzzles and other activities requiring construction or manipulation. Two children "write" on a flannel board, using letters kept in alphabetical stacks in a box. They return the letters so they fit exactly over their counterparts. Ms. Mercer praises them for neatness. She instructs them to return to their previously assigned groups as Sara enters the room.

The students are seated at six tables, four students at each table. Ms. Mercer explains, "Tables one and two will work on reading first, while tables three and four will solve math problems, and tables five and six will draw page illustrations for your collaborative Big Book. After twenty-five minutes, the groups will stop the first activity and begin working on a second task without changing seats. Twenty-five minutes later you will change again to work on the activity each group has not yet done. The math groups

---

Question 1: Conference with mother about lateness and tiredness and their effects on learning. School nurse—advise mother about healthful sleep. Document Sara's behavior.

Question 2: First grade is also for building self-esteem, learning responsibility, beginning higher-order thinking skills, and dealing with the "whole child."

Question 2: Could praise students for something more demanding than neatness—beginning to "write."

Question 4: Puzzles and other manipulatives are good for this age, as is "writing" on flannel board.

Question 3:

- Could shorten the activity time
- Could have them move seats between activities
- Could make directions and expectations clearer

and those doing illustrations will hand in their work when time is called. I will work with the two groups who are reading aloud." She plans to monitor progress of students in the reading group.

Sara is at table one. Ms. Mercer begins with this table and table two, working on reading. Several children read aloud. Ms. Mercer praises them. When Ms. Mercer calls on Sara, she begins reading in the wrong place. Joyce, seated next to Sara, points to where they are. Ms. Mercer says, "Sara, you would know where we are if you were paying attention." She calls on another child. Sara looks hurt, but soon starts to follow along in the book. Subsequently, Ms. Mercer calls on Sara, who now has the right place. Ms. Mercer then calls on another child.

During the math activity, Sara, yawning frequently, is the last to open her workbook and write her name. When she completes the page, she waits. She seems puzzled, although Ms. Mercer has already given directions. Sara gets up, sharpens a pencil, and returns to the wrong seat. "That's MY seat," accuses an angry boy. Sara apologizes and returns to her seat. Later, she waits to have her workbook checked. She has not torn out pages as Ms. Mercer instructed. Sara is told to "do it right." Sara has not creased the paper as Ms. Mercer demonstrated, so the pages do not tear out easily. Sara sucks her thumb and holds her ear for a minute. Suddenly, she yanks the paper and the pages come out with jagged edges. She receives three dots for her work. Ms. Mercer says, "Sara, this is good. I wish you could earn four dots" (the maximum). Sara slaps herself on the forehead.

During the illustration activity, Sara helps several others who have trouble thinking of ideas. Sara's illustration is among the best handed in.

Question 6: Hypothesis: ADHD?

Question 6:
- Physical/emotional problems?
- K-1 instruction so different she can't follow?
- Sara angry?—what about?
- Sara needs positive reinforcement?

Question 4: Connecting a writing activity to the field trip is good; questioning and prompting during the discussion is also good.

Question 5:

- Groups revise for another group of students, provide more information, share, present orally—writing, speaking, listening.

- Writing revision lesson—brainstorm ideas for specific part of story, rewrite.

- Pictures or discussion to identify more objects; revise, read aloud—writing, listening, speaking.

Question 6: Note hypotheses must be in addition to lack of sleep.

After the group work, Ms. Mercer places a large pad on an easel and says, "Now we're going to write about our trip to the art museum yesterday. Raise your hand and tell me something you saw or did in the museum." No one responds. She says, "Tell me the first thing we did at the museum." Sara raises her hand, offering a first sentence. After each response, Ms. Mercer asks, "What happened next?" or "What did we see next?" She prints each child's contribution.

Our Trip to the Art Museum

We rode the elevator to the second floor. We looked at different shapes on the ceiling. We saw a statue with a white triangle. We went to another room where we saw some pictures. We rode back down to the first floor. On our way out, we saw a painting of a grandfather and a boy.

During the writing of the group story, Sara fidgets in her seat, stares out the window, and makes a face at her neighbor.

Post-observation interview notes

Ms. Mercer says, "Sara is a top performer in academic achievement and on standardized tests, consistently scoring among the top five students in the class. She's so bright. It's a shame she's late and distracted so much." The mentor replies, "There may be something else bothering Sara. Although easily distracted, there may be other explanations for her behavior. Let's talk more."

These two versions of the same student-based case show that you should be well prepared to respond to each of the questions by following these steps:

- Read each case carefully, raising questions about each section as you read.

- After reading the questions, reread the section and make notes.

These questions call on your knowledge of effective teaching and learning as conceptualized in the content categories and also on theories that support teaching and learning. With this foundation of knowledge, and careful reading and annotation of the case, you should find that each of the questions can be responded to fully.

Second sample case using the content-category approach

Below is a second case, this time a document-based, teacher-based case. It is presented first using the first expert strategy—reading and annotating with questions based on the major content categories covered in the test.

MS. RILEY

Scenario

Ms. Riley is a third-year teacher in an urban elementary school. She has a heterogeneously mixed class of twenty-six 9 and 10 year olds. At the beginning of the second month of school, she introduces a long-term project called "Literature Logs." She plans the project to support her long-term goals. The following documents relate to that project.

> What information is given in this section that might be relevant to Ms. Riley's instruction?

Document 1

Literature Log Project Plan

Long-term goals:

1. Improve reading, writing, speaking, and listening abilities

2. Develop critical-thinking skills

3. Address students' individual differences

4. Build a positive classroom community

> What details about the planning might be significant?
> - Appropriateness of goals and objectives?
> - Strengths and weaknesses of the assignment?
> - Strengths and weaknesses of assessment?
> - Match of goals and objectives, activities, and assessment?
> - Ways to expand or build on goals and objectives beyond the assignment?

Objectives:

1. Students will use writing to link aspects of a text with experiences and people in their own lives.

2. Students will write accurate summaries of what they have read.

Project assignment:

Independent Reading Assignment Literature Logs

You are expected to read independently for about two hours each week (25 to 30 minutes every school night).

You may choose the book.

You are also expected to write four entries in your literature logs every two weeks.

Each entry should be about one handwritten page in your log.

At the beginning of each entry you are to write the following:

- the title and author of the book you are reading
- the numbers of the pages you are writing about
- a summary of the part of the book you have just read

In addition to writing a summary, you are also to include one or more of the following:

- similar things that have happened in your life
- what you think might happen next in the story
- dilemmas the characters are facing and how they solve them or how you would solve them

HAPPY READING!

Assessment:

Each week, each student's literature log will be assessed on the following criteria:

- Number of pages read during week
- Number of entries in literature log during week
- Ability to write effective summaries of what has been read

Document 2

Entries from Sharon's literature log and Ms. Riley's comments

Sharon
October 13, 2002
pp. 240–267

Beth died. I almost didn't notice because the book didn't really say she died. The way I noticed was because they started talking about how everyone missed her humming when she did housework and how she played the piano and all kinds of things. My mother explained to me about <u>yufasisms</u>, which are words people use for things they really don't like to talk about.

I think you are reading *Little Women* by Louisa May Alcott. Remember to state the book title, author, and pages read every time.

euphemisms

Well, we don't like to talk about it either but we say died. My aunt came to live with us because she was very sick and last year she died. I wonder what it felt like. I wonder how she felt when she was <u>dieing</u>? I miss her lots of times too.

I'm sorry.
dying

Sharon
October 27, 2002
Little Women
by Louisa May Alcott
pp. 268–296

Sharon—
I'm disappointed with your spelling in this entry in your log. You need to be more careful.

Jo <u>realy likd</u> to write and she started selling her stories to the <u>newspapper</u>. But one of her <u>frends didnt</u> like that kind of story so she <u>stoped</u> signing her name.

really liked
newspaper
friends didn't
stopped

Don't you have any thoughts about your own life to add?

- Why are there two different entries? Are there changes?
- Do the entries meet the assignment and/or the goals and objectives?
- Why are the teacher's comments given?

- What does the conversation show about Kenny as a learner?
- How does Ms. Riley interact with Kenny?
- How might Ms. Riley address Kenny as a learner based on what is learned?

Document 3

A conversation with Kenny

Ms. Riley: Kenny, in my grade book I noticed I don't have a check for your literature logs. But I'm sure you've been reading, since I've seen you read at least two books a week since the beginning of the year.

Kenny: Yeah, I read three books last week.

Ms. Riley: I noticed how much you enjoyed one of them, at least you were laughing as you read during silent reading. Did you choose one you wanted to write about in your literature log?

Kenny: Well, right now I'm reading an interesting one that takes place in a museum.

Ms. Riley: Oh, what book is that?

Kenny: It's a long name, *From the Mixed-Up Files of Mrs. Basil E. Frankenweiler.* I just started it last night.

Ms. Riley: Oh, I know that book. It's very good.

Kenny: Great, because I have a question about it.

Ms. Riley: Is it a question that could help with your reading?

Kenny: Well, someone keeps explaining things to Saxonberg and I don't know who is explaining. I don't know who Saxonberg is either.

Ms. Riley: You know, Kenny, I think if you read a few more chapters you will probably find out, and then you can write about it in your lit log.

Kenny: Well, I can tell you about it tomorrow. It has a long name, but it's a small book. I'll finish it tonight.

Ms. Riley: Well, I'd really love to see it written in your lit log or I won't be able to fill in that you've completed your homework.

Kenny: That's O.K.—I don't read to get credit. I just read for fun.

The second sample case again, using the approach of studying the questions first

Questions related to the case about Ms. Riley

1. Review Document 1, the Literature Log Project Plan. The plan demonstrates both strengths and weaknesses.

    ■   Identify ONE strength and ONE weakness of the Literature Log Project Plan.

    ■   Describe how each strength or weakness you identified demonstrates a strength or weakness in planning instruction. Base your response on principles of effective instructional planning.

2. Review Sharon's first entry (dated October 13) in Document 2, her literature log. Suppose that Ms. Riley wants to evaluate how well the entry demonstrates achievement of her long-term goals and/or her objectives.

    ■   Identify TWO aspects of Sharon's October 13 entry in her literature log that an effective evaluation would identify as achieving one or more of Ms. Riley's goals and/or her objectives.

    ■   For each aspect you identified, explain how it demonstrates achievement of one or more of Ms. Riley's goals and/or her objectives. Base your response on principles of effective assessment and evaluation.

3. In Document 2, Sharon's literature log, there are significant differences between Sharon's entry dated October 13 and her entry dated October 27. It appears that Sharon is having less success meeting the objectives for the project in the October 27 entry than in the October 13 entry.

    ■   Identify TWO significant differences between the first and second entries that indicate that Sharon is having less success in meeting the objectives of the project in the second entry.

    ■   For each difference you identified, suggest how Ms. Riley might have responded differently to Sharon in order to help Sharon continue to meet the objectives of the project. Base your response on principles of communication, assessment, and/or effective instruction.

4. In Document 3, Kenny's conversation with Ms. Riley, Kenny reveals characteristics of himself as a learner that could be used to support his development of literacy skills.

    ■   Identify ONE characteristic of Kenny as a learner and then suggest ONE strategy Ms. Riley might use to address that characteristic in a way that will support his development of literacy skills.

    ■   Describe how the strategy you suggested addresses the characteristic of Kenny as a learner and how the strategy could support Kenny's development of literacy skills. Base your response on principles of varied instructional strategies for different learners and of human development.

5. Review Ms. Riley's long-term goals at the beginning of Document 1, the Literature Log Project Plan.

   ■ Select TWO long-term goals and for each goal, identify one strategy Ms. Riley might use to expand the literature log unit beyond the stated assignment and assessment plan to address the goal.

   ■ Explain how the use of each strategy you identified could expand the literature log unit to address the selected goal. Base your response on principles of planning instruction and/or language development and acquisition.

6. Review the two objectives of the Literature Log Project Plan included in Document 1. Suppose that at the end of the project, as a culminating activity, Ms. Riley wants her students to use their literature logs to help them do a self-assessment of the two objectives.

   ■ For each of the TWO project objectives described in Document 1, suggest one assignment Ms. Riley could give the students that would serve as a self-assessment.

   ■ For each assignment you suggested, describe how Ms. Riley's students could use it as a self-assessment. Base your response on principles of effective assessment.

With these questions in mind, reread the text of the case and note marginal comments that would directly help in responding to the questions.

Questions 1 and 5: in evaluating project plan and ways to expand the unit, bear in mind the following:

- urban elementary
- heterogeneous
- 26 nine/ten year-olds
- second month of school

Question 1:

Strengths

- Independent reading two hours per week—strengthens reading skills, literacy
- Student choice of book—individual differences
- Four entries per week—writing practice, known topic
- Including summary—meets objective, builds specific writing/thinking skills
- Link to lives—student-based instruction
- Prediction—builds thinking skills
- Dilemmas of characters—thinking skills, individual differences

Weaknesses

- Assessing number of pages—unimportant, doesn't meet any objectives
- Assessing number of entries per week doesn't meet objectives, suggests low-level expectations

MS. RILEY

Scenario

Ms. Riley is a third-year teacher in an urban elementary school. She has a heterogeneously mixed class of twenty-six 9 and 10 year olds. At the beginning of the second month of school, she introduces a long-term project called "Literature Logs." She plans the project to support her long-term goals. The following documents relate to that project.

Document 1

Literature Log Project Plan

Long-term goals:

1. Improve reading, writing, speaking, and listening abilities

2. Develop critical-thinking skills

3. Address students' individual differences

4. Build a positive classroom community

Objectives:

1. Students will use writing to link aspects of a text with experiences and people in their own lives.

2. Students will write accurate summaries of what they have read.

Project Assignment:

**Independent Reading Assignment
Literature Logs**

You are expected to read independently for about two hours each week (25 to 30 minutes every school night).

You may choose the book.

You are also expected to write four entries in your literature log every two weeks.

Each entry should be about one handwritten page in your log.

At the beginning of each entry you are to write the following:

- the title and author of the book you are reading

- the numbers of the pages you are writing about

- a summary of the part of the book you have just read

In addition to writing a summary, you are also to include one or more of the following:

- similar things that have happened in your life

- what you think might happen next in the story

- dilemmas the characters are facing and how they solve them or how you would solve them

HAPPY READING!

Assessment:

Each week, each student's literature log will be assessed on the following criteria:

- Number of pages read during week

- Number of entries in literature log during week

- Ability to write effective summaries of what has been read

- Objective of building positive community never addressed

- Assessment doesn't match goals/objectives except for summaries—no critical thinking, individual differences, positive community, using writing to link reading and personal experience

Question 5:

- Speaking/listening: report aloud, students listen and question

- Critical thinking: rubric for self and teacher assessment

- Positive community: cooperative groups to share

- Individual differences: find ways students differ

- All skills: folders, students present two favorites, revise in response to input

Question 6:

- For Objective 1, could have class develop a rubric together for evaluating entries in terms of linking with personal experience—students use rubric to evaluate selected entries

- For Objective 2, could have each student write an essay about strengths and weaknesses they see in five or six of their own summaries.

Document 2

Entries from Sharon's literature log and Ms. Riley's comments.

Question 2:

- Uses critical thinking to figure out Beth is dead.

- Uses mother's definition connecting to family.

- Writes accurate brief summary.

- Wrestles with dilemma: what is it like to die?

- Strong personal voice: individual differences

Question 3:

- Oct. 27 entry, no dilemmas of characters. Positive comment in Oct. 13 entry might have encouraged more

- Oct. 27 entry, no reference to own life.

- Oct. 27 entry, no speculation; needed positive comment in Oct. 13 entry from teacher to encourage more

- Oct. 27 entry is a short summary; no critical thinking. Positive reinforcement on Oct. 13 needed

- Oct. 27 entry minimal; comments on Oct. 13 entry almost all on routine requirements and not on accurate summary or personal response

Sharon
October 13, 2002
pp. 240–267

Beth died. I almost didn't notice because the book didn't really say she died. The way I noticed was because they started talking about how everyone missed her humming when she did housework and how she played the piano and all kinds of things. My mother explained to me about <u>yufamisms</u>, which are words people use for things they really don't like to talk about.

I think you are reading *Little Women* by Louisa May Alcott. Remember to state the book title, author and pages read every time.

euphemisms

Well, we don't like to talk about it either but we say died. My aunt came to live with us because she was very sick and last year she died. I wonder what it felt like. I wonder how she felt when she was <u>dieing</u>? I miss her lots of times too.

I'm sorry.

dying

Sharon
October 27, 2002
Little Women
by Louisa May Alcott
pp. 268–296

Sharon—
I'm disappointed with your spelling in this entry in your log. You need to be more careful.

Jo <u>realy likd</u> to write and she started selling her stories to the <u>newspapper</u>. But one of her <u>frends didnt</u> like that kind of story so she <u>stoped</u> signing her name.

really liked

newspaper

friends didn't

stopped

Don't you have any thoughts about your own life to add?

Document 3

A conversation with Kenny

Ms. Riley: Kenny, in my grade book I noticed I don't have a check for your literature logs. But I'm sure you've been reading, since I've seen you read at least two books a week since the beginning of the year.

Kenny: Yeah, I read three books last week.

Ms. Riley: I noticed how much you enjoyed one of them, at least—you were laughing as you read during silent reading. Did you choose one you wanted to write about in your literature log?

Kenny: Well, right now I'm reading an interesting one that takes place in a museum.

Ms. Riley: Oh, what book is that?

Kenny: It's a long name, *From the Mixed-Up Files of Mrs. Basil E. Frankenweiler.* I just started it last night.

Ms. Riley: Oh, I know that book. It's very good.

Kenny: Great, because I have a question about it.

Ms. Riley: Is it a question that could help with your reading?

Kenny: Well, someone keeps explaining things to Saxonberg and I don't know who is explaining. I don't know who Saxonberg is either.

Ms. Riley: You know, Kenny, I think if you read a few more chapters you will probably find out, and then you can write about it in your lit log.

Kenny: Well, I can tell you about it tomorrow. It has a long name, but it's a small book. I'll finish it tonight.

Ms. Riley: Well, I'd really love to see it written in your lit log. Or I won't be able to fill in that you've completed your homework.

Kenny: That's O.K.—I don't read to get credit. I just read for fun.

Question 4:

- Loves to read; doesn't waste time writing about it—make writing more creative or provide alternate response mode like taping.

- Loves to read—ask to imitate book he likes to write own story.

- Loves to read—review favorites for other students.

- Insightful, curious reader—suggest reviews he might read to see how others respond.

- Enthusiastic about books—act out a scene from favorite for others.

- Curious mind—use the Internet for articles with interesting facts about books he likes.

With these strategies in mind, you may now want to go on to Chapter 5, which takes a different focus: writing your answers to questions based on cases.

Chapter 5
How to Answer Constructed-Response Questions

▶ ▶ ▶ ▶ ▶ ▶ ▶ ▶ ▶ ▶ ▶ ▶

How to Answer Constructed-Response Questions

The goal of this chapter is to provide you with background information, advice from experts, and close examination of sample questions and responses so that you can improve your skills in writing short answers ("constructed-response" answers) to the questions related to case studies. In the last chapter, you were given strategies for how to read, analyze, and take notes on case studies and how to relate each question to a particular section or concept in the case study. This chapter focuses on producing your response—making sure you understand what the question is asking and then using advice from experts to formulate a successful response.

How the Tests Are Scored

As you build your skills in writing answers to constructed-response questions, it is important to have in mind the process used to score the tests. If you understand where your test goes and how experts award your scores, you may have a better context in which to think about your strategies for success.

After each test administration, test books are returned to ETS. The multiple-choice answer sheets are scored using scanning machines, and the pages on which constructed-response answers appear are bundled and sent to the location of the "scoring session."

The scoring session usually takes place over two, three, or four days, depending on how many tests need to be scored. The sessions are led by "scoring leaders," highly qualified educators who have many years' experience scoring test questions. All of the remaining scorers are experienced teachers and teacher-educators. There is an effort to balance experienced scorers with newer scorers at each session; the experienced scorers provide continuity with past sessions, and the new scorers ensure that new ideas and perspectives are considered, and that the pool of scorers remains large enough to cover the test's needs throughout the year.

Preparing to train the scorers

The scoring leaders meet several days before the scoring session to assemble the materials for the training portions of the main session. Training scorers is a rigorous process, and it is designed to ensure that each response gets a score that is consistent both with the scores given to other papers and with the overall scoring philosophy and criteria established for the test when it was first designed.

The scoring leaders first review the "General Scoring Guide," which contains the overall criteria, stated in general terms, for awarding a response the score of 2, 1, or 0. The leaders also review and discuss—and make additions to, if necessary—the "Question-Specific Scoring Guides," which serve as applications of the general guide to each specific question on the test. The question-specific guides cannot cover every possible response the scorers will see, but they are designed to give enough examples to guide the scorers in making accurate judgments about the variety of answers they will encounter.

To begin identifying appropriate training materials for an individual question, the scoring leaders first read through many responses from the bundles of responses to get a sense of the range of answers. They then choose a set of "benchmarks," one paper at each score level (2, 1, and 0). These benchmarks serve as solid representative examples at each score level and are considered the foundation for score standards throughout the session.

The scoring leaders then choose a larger set of test-taker responses to serve as "sample" papers. These sample papers represent a wide variety of possible responses that the scorers might see. The sample papers will serve as the basis for practice-scoring at the scoring session, so that the scorers can "rehearse" how they will apply the scoring criteria before they begin.

The process of choosing a set of benchmark responses and a set of sample responses is followed systematically for each question to be scored at the session. After the scoring leaders are done with their selections and discussions, the sets they have chosen are photocopied and inserted into the scorers' folders in preparation for the session.

Training at the main scoring session

At the scoring session, the scorers are seated at tables of 8–12 people, with new scorers distributed about equally across all tables. One of the scoring leaders sits at each table. The "Chief Reader" is the person who has overall authority over the scoring session and plays a variety of key roles in training and in ensuring consistent and fair scores.

For each set of questions related to a case study, the training session proceeds the same way:

1. All scorers carefully read through the case study and the related questions in the test book.

2. All scorers review the General Scoring Guide and the Question-Specific Scoring Guides for the case.

3. The leaders guide the scorers through the set of benchmark responses, explaining in detail why each response received the score it did. Scorers are encouraged to ask questions and share their perspectives.

4. Scorers practice on the set of samples chosen by the leaders. At each table, the leader polls the scorers on what scores they awarded and then leads a discussion to ensure that there is a consensus about the scoring criteria and how they are to be applied.

5. When the leaders are confident that the scorers will apply the criteria consistently and accurately, the actual scoring begins.

Quality-control processes

There are a number of procedures that are designed to ensure that accuracy of scoring is maintained during the scoring session.

- One way of maintaining scoring accuracy is through "back-reading." Throughout the session, the leader at each table checks a random sample of scores awarded by scorers at the table. If the leader finds that a scorer is not applying the scoring criteria appropriately, that scorer is given more training.

- The scorers' accuracy levels are also evaluated by the scoring leaders each day by means of a computer-generated record of scores each scorer awards. This record shows how often the scorer agreed with other scorers and the average score he or she awarded for each question.

- Finally, the scoring session is designed so that many different readers contribute to any single test-taker's score. This minimizes the effects of a scorer who might score slightly more rigorously or generously than other scorers.

The entire scoring process—standardized benchmarks and samples, general and specific scoring guides, back-reading, scorer statistics, and rotation of exams to a variety of scorers—is applied consistently and systematically at every scoring session to ensure comparable scores for each administration and across all administrations of the test.

Advice from the Experts

Scorers who have scored thousands of real tests were asked to give advice to students taking the *Principles of Learning and Teaching* test. The scorers' advice boiled down to five central—and practical—pieces of advice.

1. **Answer all parts of the question.** This seems simple, but many test-takers fail to provide a complete response. If the question asks for two activities, don't forget the second one. If the question asks for a strength and a weakness, don't describe just a weakness. No matter how well you write about one activity or about a weakness, the scorers will not award you full credit.

2. **Show that you understand the pedagogical concepts related to the question.** This is a more subtle piece of advice. The scorers are looking to see not only that you can read the case study and make good observations, but also that you can relate those good observations to pedagogical concepts such as the principles of human development, the principles of motivation, the principles of effective instructional design, and the principles of diagnostic and evaluative assessment. You can show you understand these concepts not by merely mentioning that the concepts exist, but by relating them to the specifics of your response. For example, in answering a question about identifying a weakness in a teacher's approach to assessment, instead of stating that "Mr. Taft didn't give the students very good tests," you could improve on this answer and state instead, "Given that assessment of student performance is most effective when evidence is gathered frequently and through a variety of exercises and assignments, Mr. Taft's reliance on end-of-chapter tests did not give students like Paige adequate opportunities to demonstrate achievement."

3. **Show that you have a thorough understanding of the case.** Some answers receive partial credit because they are vague—they address the issues brought up in the case study at too general a level rather than at a level that takes into consideration the particulars given about a teacher, student, or assignment. If you are asked, for example, about the boy in the case study with learning disabilities whose patterns of behavior are described specifically in several sentences in the case study, don't answer the question in terms of children with disabilities in general, but, instead, focus on the boy and all the particulars you know about him.

4. **Support your answers with details.** This advice overlaps, to some extent, with numbers two and three above. The scorers are looking for some justification of your answers. If you are asked to state a "strength" shown by the teacher in a case study, don't just state the strength in a few words. Write why this is a strength—perhaps because of a particular principle of effective instructional design, which you should briefly summarize, or perhaps because of a good outcome described in the case, to which you should refer.

5. **Do not change the question or challenge the basis of the question.** Stay focused on the question that is asked and do your best to answer it. You will receive no credit or, at best, a low score if you choose to answer another question or you state that, for example, there really aren't any activities that could be proposed, or there aren't any strengths to mention, or in some other way deny the basis of the question.

The General Scoring Guide for the *Principles of Learning and Teaching* tests

The following guide provides the overarching framework that guides how constructed-response questions on the Principles of Learning and Teaching tests are scored and the method by which the Question-Specific Scoring Guide for each question is created and revised.

Principles of Learning and Teaching General Scoring Guide

All questions will be scored on a 0, 1, 2 scale.

A response that receives a score of score 2:

- Demonstrates a thorough understanding of the aspects of the case that are relevant to the question

- Responds appropriately (see next page) to all parts of the question

- If an explanation is required, provides a strong explanation that is well supported by relevant evidence

- Demonstrates a strong knowledge of pedagogical concepts, theories, facts, procedures, or methodologies relevant to the question

A response that receives a score of 1:

- Demonstrates a basic understanding of the aspects of the case that are relevant to the question

- Responds appropriately (see next page) to one portion of the question

- If an explanation is required, provides a weak explanation that is well supported by relevant evidence

- Demonstrates a some knowledge of pedagogical concepts, theories, facts, procedures, or methodologies relevant to the question

A response that received a score of 0:

- Demonstrates misunderstanding of the aspects of the case that are relevant to the question

- Fails to respond appropriately (see next page) to the question

- Is not supported by relevant evidence

- Demonstrates a little knowledge of pedagogical concepts, theories, facts, procedures, or methodologies relevant to the question

No credit is given for blank or off-topic response.

The criteria for evaluating whether a response is "appropriate" or not are established through a "model answers" methodology, which consists of the following steps:

- After a case and questions are written, three or four knowledgeable experts are asked to read the case and answer the questions, addressing each question exactly as it is worded. These experts are carefully chosen to represent the diverse perspectives and situations relevant to the testing population.

- The case writer uses these "model answers" to develop a Question-Specific Scoring Guide for each question, creating a list of specific examples that would receive full credit. This list is considered to contain *examples* of correct answers, not all the possible correct answers.

- These question-specific scoring guides based on model answers provide the basis for choosing the papers that serve as benchmark and sample papers for the purpose of training the scorers at the scoring session.

- During the scoring sessions, while reading student papers, scorers can add new answers to the scoring guide as they see fit.

- Training at the scoring session is aimed to ensure that scorers do not score papers on the basis of their opinions or their own preferences but rather make judgments based on the carefully established criteria in the scoring guide.

A closer look at twelve questions

Given this information about how constructed-response responses are scored and what the scorers are looking for in successful responses, you can now more thoroughly examine the questions you read for the first time concerning two cases presented in chapter 4 and practice on them. When you read a question for the first time, it is helpful to think about what the question is really asking and then to think about which of the content categories the question assesses. Note in the samples below that the last sentence of each question contains a reference to the content category addressed. This is nearly always the case in the constructed-response questions on the *Principles of Learning and Teaching* test, although there may be instances when the category is not explicitly stated.

As you plan and evaluate your response to the question, think about the scoring criteria used by the scorers, and think about the advice given by the experts.

The two cases and twelve practice questions, with accompanying advice and commentary, begin on the next page.

Here is the case entitled "Sara" that you read in chapter 4.

SARA

Scenario

Six-year-old Sara lives with her mother, who has a relaxed schedule. Ms. Mercer, Sara's teacher, notes that Sara is often tired and inattentive after arriving late. Sara says she frequently stays up past midnight if others are up. Ms. Mercer, a second-year teacher, has asked her mentor to observe Sara and suggest ways to help Sara achieve Ms. Mercer's purposes.

Observation: Ms. Mercer's Class, April 30

Pre-observation interview notes

Ms. Mercer says, "The purposes of first grade are to teach children 'school survival skills' and reading, writing, and arithmetic." She adds, "Sara needs help with 'survival skills,' including following directions, concentrating on a task to its completion, and being attentive to the lessons I present."

Mentor classroom observation—focus on Sara Porter

As Ms. Mercer's class begins, the children play with puzzles and other activities requiring construction or manipulation. Two children "write" on a flannel board, using letters kept in alphabetical stacks in a box. They return the letters so they fit exactly over their counterparts. Ms. Mercer praises them for neatness. She instructs them to return to their previously assigned groups as Sara enters the room.

The students are seated at six tables, four students at each table. Ms. Mercer explains, "Tables one and two will work on reading first, while tables three and four will solve math problems, and tables five and six will draw page illustrations for your collaborative Big Book. After twenty-five minutes, the groups will stop the first activity and begin working on a second task without changing seats. Twenty-five minutes later, you will change again to work on the activity each group has not yet done. The math groups and those doing illustrations will hand in their work when time is called. I will work with the two groups who are reading aloud." She plans to monitor progress of students in the reading group.

Sara is at table one. Ms. Mercer begins with this table and table two, working on reading. Several children read aloud. Ms. Mercer praises them. When Ms. Mercer calls on Sara, she begins reading in the wrong place. Joyce, seated next to Sara, points to where they are. Ms. Mercer says, "Sara, you would know where we are if you were paying attention." She calls on another child. Sara looks hurt, but soon starts to follow along in the book. Subsequently, Ms. Mercer calls on Sara, who now has the right place. Ms. Mercer then calls on another child.

During the math activity, Sara, yawning frequently, is the last to open her workbook and write her name. When she completes the page, she waits. She seems puzzled, although Ms. Mercer has already given directions. Sara gets up, sharpens a pencil, and returns to the wrong seat. "That's MY seat," accuses an angry boy. Sara apologizes and returns to her seat. Later, she waits to have her workbook checked. She has not torn out pages as Ms. Mercer instructed. Sara is told to "do it right." Sara has not creased the paper as Ms. Mercer demonstrated, so the pages do not tear out easily. Sara sucks her thumb and holds her ear for a minute. Suddenly, she yanks the paper and the pages come out with jagged edges. She receives three dots for her work. Ms. Mercer says, "Sara, this is good. I wish you could earn four dots" (the maximum). Sara slaps herself on the forehead.

During the illustration activity, Sara helps several others who have trouble thinking of ideas. Sara's illustration is among the best handed in.

After the group work, Ms. Mercer places a large pad on an easel and says, "Now we're going to write about our trip to the art museum yesterday. Raise your hand and tell me something you saw or did in the museum." No one responds. She says, "Tell me the first thing we did at the museum." Sara raises her hand, offering a first sentence. After each response, Ms. Mercer asks, "What happened next?" or "What did we see next?" She prints each child's contribution.

Our Trip to the Art Museum

We rode the elevator to the second floor. We looked at different shapes on the ceiling. We saw a statue with a white triangle. We went to another room where we saw some pictures. We rode back down to the first floor. On our way out, we saw a painting of a grandfather and a boy.

During the writing of the group story, Sara fidgets in her seat, stares out the window, and makes a face at her neighbor.

Post-observation interview notes

Ms. Mercer says, "Sara is a top performer in academic achievement and on standardized tests, consistently scoring among the top five students in the class. She's so bright. It's a shame she's late and distracted so much." The mentor replies, "There may be something else bothering Sara. Although she is easily distracted, there may be other explanations for her behavior. Let's talk more."

Consider the first question related to the case study entitled "Sara" that you read and analyzed in Chapter 4 and complete the exercises below it. These are designed to help you think critically about what is being asked.

Question 1

1. **Suppose that Ms. Mercer and her mentor discuss how to connect school and Sara's home environment for the benefit of Sara's learning.**

   - **Identify TWO specific actions Ms. Mercer might take to connect school and Sara's home environment for the benefit of Sara's learning.**

   - **Explain how each action you identified could benefit Sara's learning. Base your response on principles of fostering school-parent relationships to support student learning.**

Think about what is being asked.

In the space below, state in your own words what you think the question is asking.

Compare your impression of what is being asked with the explanation below.

The question asks for

- *two* things Ms. Mercer might do to help the school and parent work together to identify Sara's needs

- for *each* thing, an explanation of how it could help Sara's learning

Think about the category being assessed.

- The larger community

The important aspect of this content category is fostering "relationships with ... parents." Also, although they are not the focus of the question, you need to understand the underlying human development issues—the physical, social, emotional, moral, and cognitive development of children this age. Both aspects (fostering relationships ... and human development) are critical in a teacher's responsibilities to meet the needs of all students, but especially students like Sara.

Write your response

In the space below, write what you consider to be a response that directly addresses the question.

Reflect on your response in light of the scoring guide, sample responses, and commentary.

Note that the scoring guide that will be used to evaluate responses to this question specifies two actions and that they must be *appropriate*. Note that the rubric contains bulleted possible answers, but that they are introduced by the statement "...such as the following." The list is neither prescriptive nor restrictive; all *appropriate* responses are given full credit. The experienced educators who score the test can evaluate the appropriateness of responses that are not contained in this list.

Scoring Guide for Question 1

Score of 2

The response presents two appropriate actions Ms. Mercer might take to connect school and Sara's home environment and explanations of how each could benefit Sara's learning, such as the following:

- Ms. Mercer can seek a conference with Sara's mother to determine why Sara often arrives late and appears tired in class. Together they can discuss strategies to address Sara's problems.

- Ms. Mercer might ask the school nurse to schedule a conference with Sara, her mother, and Ms. Mercer to explore the reasons for Sara's tiredness in class. With the mediation of the school nurse, the adults and Sara can discuss ways to improve Sara's attentiveness and ability to follow directions.

- Ms. Mercer might telephone Sara's mother and explain that Sara is doing very well on tests, but that she is falling behind in class because she arrives late, appears very tired, reports she often stays up late, and finds it hard to follow directions or to contribute to discussions in class. Together they can explore ways to address Sara's problematic behavior.

- Ms. Mercer can document one or two weeks of Sara's inability to follow directions or to arrive on time and then call Sara's mother or schedule a conference to discuss what can be done at home and in school to improve Sara's ability to follow directions and to arrive on time.

- Ms. Mercer could gather a few articles about the necessity of at least eight hours of sleep each night for six-year-olds. She could ask for a conference with Sara's mother and discuss with her the harmful effects Sara's apparent lack of sleep is having on her school performance. Together they can seek solutions to Sara's tiredness.

- Ms. Mercer can discuss with second- and third-grade teachers the importance of a students' ability to follow directions and to contribute in class. She could then seek a conference with Sara's mother to show the negative effects of Sara's inability to follow directions and contribute in class, indicating why that might be important for her present and future well-being.

Score of 1

The response presents two appropriate actions Ms. Mercer might take to connect school and Sara's home environment for the benefit of Sara's learning, without sufficient explanations, or presents one appropriate action with explanation, such as those presented in score point 2.

Score of 0

The response fails to address the question, presents inappropriate actions, or is vague.

Response that would receive a score of 2.

First, Ms. Mercer can collect as much information as possible to use in conferences with Sara's mother to help establish a positive relationship and to help identify Sara's strengths and needs. Ms. Mercer should do some systematic observation and objective description of Sara's performance and the effects of her late arrival and inattentiveness in class. Observation information should also include Sara's good qualities. She might also gather information, with the help of the school nurse, about healthful habits for children Sara's age, including amount of sleep needed. Second, Ms. Mercer then needs to seek a parent conference in order to discuss the areas in which Sara shows strengths as a student and to address her concerns about Sara's performance in class. By showing a sincere interest in Sara's positive growth and development as well as identifying the youngster's problems, Ms. Mercer can work to establish a positive working relationship with Sara's mother.

Commentary on the above response

The response presents two appropriate actions in considerable detail. The actions are related to each other, but are still clearly two separate steps in building a positive home-school relationship. The actions are clearly presented and directly applicable to the situation. The response receives full credit.

Response that would receive a score of 1.

Ms. Mercer needs to talk with Sara's mother in order to connect school and Sara's home environment for the benefit of Sara's learning. She should call her to make an appointment, and when Sara's mother comes to school for the meeting, they can begin to discuss Sara's behavior and the possible causes for it. In the same way, the school—Ms. Mercer and perhaps the nurse or school psychologist—know a lot about what Sara does at school and a lot of theory about child growth and development, and they can help Sara's mother understand what her problems are and how they can be approached. In this way, Sara will benefit because both home and school will know more and be better able to help her.

Commentary on the above response

The response presents only one action. Calling the mother is not presented as a separate action that, in itself, would address the problem, but rather as a preliminary to the meeting. The response does present one action that is appropriate, clearly expressed, and applicable to the situation. The response receives partial credit.

Response that would receive a score of 0.

Although it sounds like a good idea, probably very little if anything will be gained by trying to establish contact with Sara's mother. From the way Sara behaves in school, it appears that a very likely cause of her problems lies at home, especially if her mother keeps her up very late at night and has little regard for her welfare. Therefore, in the best interests of Sara, Ms. Mercer should rely on the school to help her try to figure out what's going on with Sara and how best to help her and should not involve Sara's mother.

Commentary on the above response

The response presents an inappropriate action. The INTASC standard that reads "the teacher fosters relationships with school colleagues, parents, and agencies in the larger community to support students' learning and well being" clearly indicates that deliberately not involving Sara's mother is an inappropriate course of action. The response receives no credit.

Here is the second question related to the "Sara" case.

Question 2

2. Review the pre-observation notes in which Ms. Mercer explains the purposes of first grade as she sees them. Suppose that her mentor suggests that Ms. Mercer consider other purposes of first grade and how she might modify her instruction to address those purposes and the related needs of Sara and her other students.

   - Identify TWO additional purposes of first grade that Ms. Mercer could consider when planning her instruction, in order to meet the needs of Sara and/or her other students.

   - For each purpose you identified, explain how Ms. Mercer might modify her instruction to address the purpose and meet the needs of Sara and/or her other students. Base your response on principles of planning instruction and learning theory.

Think about what is being asked:

In the space below, state in your own words what you think the question is asking.

Compare your impression of what is being asked with the explanation below.

The question asks for

- *two* additional purposes that might indicate needs of Sara and the other students

- for *each* purpose, an explanation of how Ms. Mercer might modify her instruction to meet these needs

Think about the categories being assessed.

- Planning instruction

- Learning theory

It is important to know how to establish appropriate purposes for specific groups of students, and how to plan instruction to meet those purposes in a way that will engage students fully in learning.

Write your response.

In the space below, write what you consider to be a response that directly addresses the question.

Reflect on your response in light of the scoring guide, sample responses, and commentary.

Remember as you study the scoring guide below that scorers use it as the primary means of evaluating responses, and use their professional knowledge to evaluate the appropriateness of responses. Remember, too, that the words "such as" introducing the bulleted examples of possible appropriate responses mean that these possible responses are neither prescriptive nor restrictive.

Scoring Guide for Question 2

Score of 2

The response presents two additional appropriate purposes for first grade. For each, the response offers one modification for the teacher's instruction to better meet the needs of Sara or the other students, such as the following:

- The mentor can suggest that another purpose for first grade is to build self-esteem and confidence by providing success for all students in a variety of learning situations. Instead of pointing out Sara's weaknesses, she could praise her in class when she does well. By building in opportunities for success and building self-esteem and confidence, she can increase the engagement of Sara and other students.

- The mentor can suggest that another purpose of first grade is to offer students multiple opportunities to recognize and accept their responsibilities. For example, she could have a student repeat the directions she gives to each group and could have students identify what they are responsible for doing.

- The mentor can suggest that first grade should also be about developing more challenging skills than those for "survival," and could recommend that rather than just having the students learn survival routines, Ms. Mercer could introduce higher-order tasks, including evaluation, analysis, and/or synthesis at an appropriate level for students to perform as part of each task.

- The mentor can suggest that another purpose for first grade is for students to learn to support one another in their learning. Instead of reprimanding Sara and other students for not hearing the directions the first time, she can appoint a buddy for each student so they can check with each other when they're unsure what to do.

- The mentor can suggest that another purpose of first grade is to develop "the whole child," addressing physical, emotional, and intellectual growth and development. For example, Ms. Mercer might learn more about Sara's talents, interests, and problems so she can address Sara's strengths and needs in all three areas.

Score of 1

The response presents two additional purposes, but does not explain how Ms. Mercer might modify her instruction, or presents one additional purpose and explains how she might modify her instruction, in keeping with the purposes and modifications presented in score point 2.

Score of 0

The response fails to address the question, presents inappropriate additional purposes and modifications, or is vague.

Response that would receive a score of 2.

The mentor can point out to Ms. Mercer that an important additional purpose for first grade is to address the physical, emotional, and intellectual needs of all children. She could have modified her instruction by learning more about Sara, and then addressing Sara's needs in a carefully planned way that supports Sara's growth and development. A second additional purpose for first grade is to build students' self-esteem and confidence. The mentor could point out that Ms. Mercer shows her concern about Sara to the mentor, but to Sara she generally shows her frustration and impatience with what Sara does wrong. If Ms. Mercer began by praising Sara for her ability and acknowledging her genuine contributions, she would take an important step toward building Sara's self-esteem and confidence.

Commentary on the above response

The response presents two appropriate additional purposes of first grade. For each, the response offers one modification for her instruction to better meet Sara's needs. The two purposes and the accompanying explanations of the modification are presented clearly and thoroughly. Therefore, the response receives full credit.

Response that would receive a score of 1.

One additional purpose of first grade is to begin introducing some of the higher-order thinking skills at a level appropriate for the age and grade level. Ms. Mercer is right that reading, writing, and arithmetic are important, but she could help the students grow much more effectively by helping them begin to use some synthesis, analysis, and evaluation skills in the tasks they are doing. For example, in her oral reading activity, she could ask some questions related to what the students are reading that would require them to use these higher-order thinking skills. She could ask how characters are alike, or ask them to name two things they really like about the story.

Commentary on the above response

The response presents one appropriate additional purpose for first grade and suggests an appropriate modification Ms. Mercer might make in her instruction. Both the purpose and the modification are explained with sufficient appropriate detail. However, the response does not present two additional purposes with modifications as the question requires, and so receives partial credit.

Response that would receive a score of 0.

It seems to me that, with everything first grade teachers are expected to do these days, Ms. Mercer has more than enough challenge with the purposes she has established. Yes, it might be nice if she could think of some "additional" purposes, but I think her students will be best served if she concentrates on the purposes she has established and works to give her students a solid foundation on which later grades can build.

Commentary on the above response

The response fails to address the question. Responses that argue with the premise of the question receive no credit.

Here is the third question related to the "Sara" case.

Question 3

3. **Assume that the groups working on mathematics and illustrations for the Big Book become very noisy and unproductive over the course of the activity.**

   ■ **Suggest TWO changes Ms. Mercer could have made in the planning and/or implementation of the group work that would have made the activity more successful.**

   ■ **Explain how each suggested change you suggested could have made the group work activity more successful. Base your response on principles of planning instruction and human development.**

Think about what is being asked:

In the space below, state in your own words what you think the question is asking.

Compare your impression of what is being asked with the explanation below.

The question asks for

   ■ *two* changes Ms. Mercer could have made that could have made the group work more successful

   ■ for *each* change, an explanation of how the group work would have been more successful

Think about the categories being assessed.

   ■ Planning instruction

   ■ Human development

Again, note the importance of addressing each of these two categories. These two are especially important when a teacher is thinking about planning specific instructional strategies for specific groups of students. Note again that knowledge from learning theory and human behavior and motivation should be utilized to develop strategies for organizing and supporting individual and group work.

Write your response.

In the space below, write what you consider to be a response that directly addresses the question.

Reflect on your response in light of the scoring guide, sample responses, and commentary.

Again, note that the scoring guide contains possible appropriate responses that are illustrative only and are neither prescriptive nor restrictive. Remember that there are many appropriate ways in which the question could be answered, and these are illustrations only.

Scoring Guide for Question 3

Score of 2

The response presents two appropriate changes Ms. Mercer could have made in planning and implementing the group work, and explanations of how they could make the activity more successful, such as the following:

- Ms. Mercer could shorten the amount of time for each activity, so that the students would be more likely to stay on-task. Twenty-five minutes per activity is too much time for students this age to be expected to work independently or in small groups without direct supervision.

- Ms. Mercer should teach or review group work behavior and expectations before the work begins, so that her students would be more likely to participate appropriately in the activity.

- Ms. Mercer could have groups move seats between activities. Students this age need to move more frequently and have physical activity, rather than being expected to sit in the same seats for long periods of time.

- Ms. Mercer could use parent volunteers to help support and monitor the work of the two groups with whom she is not working directly.

- Ms. Mercer could give clear directions, with steps and models of what final products are to look like, before students begin to work, so that they would be more likely to understand and achieve the objectives of the activity.

- Ms. Mercer could display posters that illustrate what students are to do; posters can also indicate the location of each group activity. The posters would provide the students with clearer directions for completing the activity.

Score of 1

The response presents two appropriate changes Ms. Mercer could have made in planning and implementing the group work without explanations of how the changes make the activity more successful, or presents one change Ms. Mercer could have made with an explanation of how the activity could have been more successful, such as those presented in score point 2.

Score of 0

The response fails to address the question, presents inappropriate ways to introduce and implement the group work, or is vague.

Response that would receive a score of 2.

First, Ms. Mercer should plan shorter times for the students to work on each activity, so that the students would be able to stay on-task. Twenty-five minutes is too long to expect students this age to work alone or even in small groups on one activity. Next, she should plan to review much more carefully what she expects students in each group to do, showing them examples of what their finished work is supposed to look like. Providing clearer expectations would increase the likelihood that the students would complete the activity as desired.

Commentary on the above response

The response presents two appropriate changes Ms. Mercer could have made in the planning and implementation of the group work. They take into account the students' developmental levels and present approaches that would strengthen the group activities. The response receives full credit.

Response that would receive a score of 1.

Ms. Mercer should introduce the activity by teaching or reviewing rules for behavior and procedures for small group work. She can't expect students to know this, or even to remember it from day to day. She needs to explain rules for working independently, or rules for working cooperatively so students can help each other without disturbing other students. If she reviews these things, the groups will have a better chance of success.

Commentary on the above response

The response presents one appropriate change Ms. Mercer could have made in her planning. It is presented in detail, but constitutes only one change. The question requires two appropriate changes; the response receives partial credit.

Response that would receive a score of 0:

Ms. Mercer should not try to use small group work with students this age. They are too young to be expected to work independently or even in small groups. She should keep the class together so that she can have direct supervision over them at all times.

Commentary on the above response

The response argues with the question, rather than responding to it in an appropriate way. Responses that argue with the premise of the question receive no credit.

Here is the fourth question related to the "Sara" case.

Question 4

4. **In the activities described in the Mentor Classroom Observation, Ms. Mercer demonstrates understanding of developmentally appropriate instruction.**

    ■ **Identify TWO strengths in the instructional approaches Ms. Mercer uses in the activities that reflect understanding of the principles of developmentally appropriate instruction.**

    ■ **Explain how each of these strengths you identified provides evidence of an understanding of the principles of developmentally appropriate instruction. Base your response on principles of planning instruction and human development.**

Think about what is being asked:

In the space below, state in your own words what you think the question is asking.

```
```

Compare your impression of what is being asked with the explanation below.

The question asks for

■ *two* strengths in Ms. Mercer's instructional approaches

■ for *each* strength, an explanation of how it demonstrates understanding of developmentally appropriate instruction

Think about the categories being assessed

■ Planning instruction

■ Human development

Again, note the importance of addressing each of these two categories. These two are especially important in thinking about planning specific instructional strategies for specific groups of students. Note again that knowledge from learning theory and human behavior and motivation are utilized to develop strategies for organizing and supporting individual and group work.

Write your response.

In the space below, write what you consider to be a response that directly addresses the question.

Reflect on your response in light of the scoring guide, sample responses, and commentary.

Scoring Guide for Question 4

Score of 2

The response presents two strengths in Ms. Mercer's instructional approaches, with evidence of understanding of developmentally appropriate instructions, such as the following:

- Having students engage in play with puzzles or other activities requiring construction and manipulation is very appropriate to the students' developmental levels

- Having the students "write" on flannel boards is an appropriate language development activity for students this age

- Having students work on a variety of tasks, rotating among three tasks, is an appropriate activity-centered approach for students this age

- Connecting the writing activity to the students' previous experience on the field trip is an appropriate way to help students this age make connections and, therefore, perform well

- Questioning and prompting students as they are developing the account of the trip is an appropriate way to help students this age develop writing fluency

Score of 1

The response presents two strengths in Ms. Mercer's instructional approaches, without appropriate discussion of how they are developmentally appropriate, or presents one strength in Ms. Mercer's instructional approach with evidence of how it is developmentally appropriate, such as those presented in score point 2.

Score of 0

The response fails to address the question, presents inappropriate points as strengths, or is vague.

Response that would receive a score of 2.

Ms. Mercer's lesson does display strengths. She is developing students' writing skills in an appropriate way for students this age by having students "write" at the flannel board. They are developing an enthusiasm for writing and a sense of what it means to put letters together to form words. Another strength is the way she connects the writing of the story to their previous trip to the museum. When teachers connect one activity to previous knowledge or experience of students, the students this age have a better opportunity to learn and demonstrate their learning. It was also a strength to prompt and question students as they were developing ideas for the story. They were having trouble remembering, but without just telling them what to say, she helped them develop ideas.

Commentary on the above response

The response presents more than two appropriate strengths. Each point presented is valid and explained in sufficient detail. No additional credit, however, is given for going beyond the requirement of the question. The response receives full credit.

Response that would receive a score of 1.

Ms. Mercer's use of rotating group activities for the students is a strength of the lesson. This activity-centered approach is very effective in helping students develop skills and remain engaged in the work. The activities are varied enough to keep the students interested and are all appropriate for students this age.

Commentary on the above response

The response presents one appropriate strength of her approach. It is explained in sufficient detail. However, the response presents only one strength, and the question calls for two. It receives partial credit.

Response that would receive a score of 0.

One appropriate strength in her approach is that she is very nice to the children. Boys and girls in first grade need lots of personal attention and a supportive classroom environment. Teachers who are enthusiastic and supportive of their students help students a lot more than teachers who are too stern and critical.

Commentary on the above response

The response refers to aspects for teaching first grade that are important. However, the discussion does not address the question of strengths of Ms. Mercer's instructional approaches. Discussing aspects of instruction stressed by the INTASC standards but not relevant to the question posed is not sufficient to receive credit.

Here is the fifth question related to the "Sara" case.

Question 5

5. Assume that the day after the lesson was observed, Ms. Mercer's objective is to use the story about the museum visit to continue building students' literacy.

   ■ Identify TWO strategies and/or activities involving the story about the museum visit that Ms. Mercer could use to continue building students' literacy.

   ■ For each strategy and/or activity you identified, explain how it could help build literacy. Base your response on principles of language development and acquisition.

Think about what is being asked.

In the space below, state in your own words what you think the question is asking.

> (blank box)

Compare your impression of what is being asked with the explanation below.

The question asks for

   ■ *two* strategies or activities the teacher could use to meet this objective

   ■ an explanation of how *each* strategy or activity helps build literacy

Think about the category being assessed.

   ■ Planning instruction

For students this age, building literacy skills is essential. The ability to address this need in practice is critical.

Write your response.

In the space below, write what you consider to be a response that directly addresses the question.

Reflect on your response in light of the scoring guide, sample responses, and commentary.

Scoring Guide for Question 5

Score of 2

The response offers two appropriate strategies Ms. Mercer could use and explains how each strategy meets her objective, such as the following:

- Ms. Mercer could tell the students their story is going to be shared with students in another class. Have them brainstorm ways to make the story more interesting for other children their age, including more information they remember that might be included. This activity would build their writing skills by adding information for a specific audience.

- Ms. Mercer could have copies of the story run off by the end of the day and give each student a copy of the story. She could ask them to have their parents read the story with them and ask questions about it. The next day they could use the questions they can remember to brainstorm more ideas. This activity would build their oral literacy through conversation with their parents and their writing skills through revision.

- Ms. Mercer can ask students to think about one thing they remember from the visit (the marble with the white triangle, the ceiling pictures, or the room full of statues) and draw a picture of it. She could post the pictures and use them as a basis for a word board of good descriptive language. This builds their writing skills by revising to add more specific, focused details about one aspect of the visit.

- Ms. Mercer might read the children a story about a visit. She could have children discuss what they liked about the story, and use this information to brainstorm ways to write about their own visit. This builds their writing skills by modeling an effective description, and their speaking and listening skills as they share aloud ideas to revise their story.

- Ms. Mercer can show pictures of the various things the class saw at the museum. By asking each group to identify an item that interests them and discuss what they could write to make another person their age interested in the item, Ms. Mercer could build on their discussion and listening skills and develop writing skills.

Score of 1

The response presents one appropriate strategy and explains how it meets the objective to develop students' literacy such as those presented in score point 2, or presents two appropriate strategies such as those presented in score point 2 but does not explain how the strategies meet the objective.

Score of 0

The response fails to address the question, presents inappropriate strategies and explanations of how the strategies meet the objective, or is vague.

Response that would receive a score of 2.

Ms. Mercer has many opportunities to develop the speaking, reading, writing, and listening skills of her students by using the description of the museum visit in creative ways. By having students revise the story for a specific audience, say a group of children their age, and describe their visit in ways that would make the others want to go to the museum too, she can increase their ability to write for a specific audience. If she were to display pictures of things they saw, ask them to provide descriptive words, and then write the words beneath the pictures, she would help them develop vocabulary appropriate to their writing and develop speaking and listening skills.

Commentary on the above response

The response identifies two specific ways in which Ms. Mercer could continue building students' literacy. The activities suggested are appropriate and described in detail. The response receives full credit.

Response that would receive a score of 1:

Ms. Mercer could use two additional activities to build students' literacy. The next day they could return to the story they have written, and could brainstorm some additional details that could be added to make the story more interesting. Ms. Mercer might have to prompt them a bit, but by giving them some hints, she could help them remember things that would make the story fuller and more detailed.

She could also develop literacy by having "listening stations" where students can listen to tape recorded stories and follow along in books. By connecting the story read aloud (on tape) and the story as it appears in print, she can help them understand that the words on the page have real meaning.

Commentary on the above response

The question specifically says her objective is "to use the story about the museum visit to continue building students' literacy" and asks for two strategies or activities to meet this objective. One of the activities presented does extend the lesson and receives credit. However, the second activity is unrelated to the story about the museum and therefore is considered unresponsive to the question. The response receives partial credit.

Response that would receive a score of 0.

I believe developing literacy is probably the most important academic objective first grade teachers can have. Literacy involves developing specifically the skills of reading, writing, speaking, and listening. There are many activities that first grade teachers can use to develop literacy. It is important to remember that for first graders, print is very confusing, and they often see little connection between ideas and print, so anything a teacher can do to help them make that connection will help.

Commentary on the above response

Merely selecting one word—even a critical word—from the question and writing about it does not constitute responding appropriately to the question. While the question does deal with developing literacy, the response does not address the specific requirements of the question and receives no credit.

Here is the sixth question related to the "Sara" case.

Question 6

6. **In the post-observation notes, Ms. Mercer's mentor suggests that they explore explanations for Sara's inattentive behavior.**

   ■ **Suggest TWO hypotheses other than lack of sleep that Ms. Mercer and her mentor might explore to learn more about why Sara behaves as she does in class.**

   ■ **For each hypothesis you suggested, describe at least one action that Ms. Mercer and her mentor might take to see if the hypothesis might be correct. Base your response on principles of human development, motivation, and diagnostic assessment.**

Think about what is being asked.

In the space below, state in your own words what you think the question is asking.

Compare your impression of what is being asked with the explanation below.

The question asks for

■ *two* hypotheses that Ms. Mercer and the mentor might explore to learn more about Sara's behavior in class

■ for *each* hypothesis, a description of one action Ms. Mercer and the mentor might take to learn more about why Sara behaves as she does

Think about the categories being assessed.

- Diagnostic and evaluative strategies in the areas of human development and learner motivation

The ability to make effective assessments, both of the needs of students and of the strengths and weaknesses in student performance, is essential. Here, the question asks for hypotheses to explore to learn more about Sara's behavior—in other words, for the beginning of a diagnostic assessment.

Write your response.

In the space below, write what you consider to be a response that directly addresses the question.

Reflect on your response in light of the scoring guide, sample responses, and commentary.

Scoring Guide for Question 6

Score of 2

The response presents two appropriate hypotheses that the mentor and Ms. Mercer can explore to learn the causes for Sara's inattentiveness in class, and for each hypothesis, the response describes one action Ms. Mercer and her mentor could take to see if the hypothesis is correct, such as the following:

- One hypothesis is that Sara has ADHD or some other learning disability. They can have the nurse or a counselor observe Sara and determine whether she needs further testing.

- One hypothesis is that there are physical or emotional factors in Sara's background that affect her behavior now. They could look for information in Sara's background data that suggests causes for her inattentiveness. They can examine Sara's folder and find out if any potential causes are listed in the data.

- One hypothesis is that Sara had a very different kind of teacher in kindergarten, and she may miss the kind of instruction with which she was familiar. Ms. Mercer and the mentor could talk with Sara's kindergarten teacher to find out what behavior patterns she exhibited and what kinds of approaches worked well with her.

- One hypothesis is that Sara is angry about something, related either to school or other areas of her life, as indicated by her angry gestures. They could explore a variety of sources including Sara's mother, Sara's records, or a discussion with Sara herself to determine if there is ongoing anger.

- One hypothesis is that Sara needs ongoing, frequent positive reinforcement in order to function well. They could try a program of greatly enhanced positive reinforcement and praise to see if Sara responds to this approach.

- One hypothesis is that Sara is bored. Ms. Mercer has noted her high test scores and identified her as very bright. She may be bored with activities that aren't challenging her. They could have a counselor or other trained staff member work with Sara to determine if she would respond to more intellectually challenging work.

Score of 1

The response presents two appropriate hypotheses that the mentor and Ms. Mercer can explore to learn the causes for Sara's inattentiveness in class, but no actions they could take to see if the hypotheses might be correct, or the response presents one appropriate hypothesis Ms. Mercer and the mentor could explore with one action they could take to see if the hypothesis might be correct, such as those presented in score point 2.

Score of 0

The response fails to address the question, presents inappropriate hypotheses, or is vague.

Response that would receive a score of 2.

The mentor may suspect that Sara has ADHD or some other learning disability that prevents her from maintaining concentration on her work. They can work with the school nurse or counselor or other professional staff to explore this possibility. The mentor may also suggest that Sara needs consistent, ongoing positive reinforcement, and performs poorly when exposed to criticism. She and Ms. Mercer could work together to provide consistent feedback to Sara that would build self-esteem and confidence, and see if this approach helps Sara be more fully engaged in the work.

Commentary on the above response

The response presents two appropriate hypotheses the mentor teacher and Ms. Mercer could explore to learn more about Sara's behavior. They are presented briefly, but are specific and presented in sufficient detail. Responses need not be lengthy nor elaborately written to receive full credit. This response does receive full credit.

Response that would receive a score of 1.

The mentor teacher and Ms. Mercer could explore the possibility that Sara has some form of a learning disability that prevents her from paying attention. They could use a school psychologist to help them make this determination.

Commentary on the above response

The response presents only one hypothesis. It is appropriate and although very brief is sufficient for partial credit.

Response that would receive a score of 0.

The mentor teacher and Ms. Mercer could look for the causes of Sara's behavior in class. The mentor teacher seems to understand that there may be more involved than Sara's lack of sleep. She can clearly help Ms. Mercer and together, they can brainstorm possibilities about what may be causes of Sara's behavior. A second thing they could do would be to consult some of the professional staff of the school and ask them for help in figuring out what's going on with Sara so they can help her.

Commentary on the above response

The response fails to address the question. A response that paraphrases the question or offers related information that does not directly address the requirements of the question receives no credit.

Look now at how the questions for the teacher-based, document-based case "Ms. Riley" might be analyzed, responded to, and evaluated. Again, the materials below are intended as illustrative of how you might prepare for practice cases and respond to actual cases. As you prepare, remember that the critical factors to bear in mind as you read and respond to the questions are *what is being asked* and the *categories being assessed.*

Here is the case entitled "Ms. Riley" that you read in Chapter 4.

Ms. Riley

Scenario

Ms. Riley is a third-year teacher in an urban elementary school. She has a heterogeneously mixed class of twenty-six 9 and 10 year olds. At the beginning of the second month of school, she introduces a long-term project called "Literature Logs." She plans the project to support her long-term goals. The following documents relate to that project.

Document 1

Literature Log Project Plan

Long-term goals:

1. Improve reading, writing, speaking, and listening abilities

2. Develop critical-thinking skills

3. Address students' individual differences

4. Build a positive classroom community

Objectives:

1. Students will use writing to link aspects of a text with experiences and people in their own lives.

2. Students will write accurate summaries of what they have read.

Project assignment:

Independent Reading Assignment
Literature Logs

You are expected to read independently for about two hours each week (25 to 30 minutes every school night).

You may choose the book.

You are also expected to write four entries in your literature logs every two weeks.

Each entry should be about one handwritten page in your log.

At the beginning of each entry you are to write the following:

- the title and author of the book you are reading

- the numbers of the pages you are writing about

- a summary of the part of the book you have just read

In addition to writing a summary, you are also to include one or more of the following:

- similar things that have happened in your life

- what you think might happen next in the story

- dilemmas the characters are facing and how they solve them or how you would solve them

HAPPY READING!

Assessment:

Each week, each student's literature log will be assessed on the following criteria:

- Number of pages read during week

- Number of entries in literature log during week

- Ability to write effective summaries of what has been read

Document 2

Entries from Sharon's literature log and Ms. Riley's comments

Sharon
October 13, 2002
pp. 240-267

Beth died. I almost didn't notice because the book didn't really say she died. The way I noticed was because they started talking about how everyone missed her humming when she did housework and how she played the piano and all kinds of things. My mother explained to me about <u>yufamisms</u>, which are words people use for things they really don't like to talk about.

I think you are reading *Little Women* by Louisa May Alcott. Remember to state the book title, author and pages read every time.

euphemisms

Well, we don't like to talk about it either but we say died. My aunt came to live with us because she was very sick and last year she died. I wonder what it felt like. I wonder how she felt when she was <u>dieing</u>? I miss her lots of times too.

I'm sorry.

dying

Sharon
October 27, 2002
Little Women
by Louisa May Alcott
pp. 268-296

Sharon—

I'm disappointed with your spelling in this entry in your log. You need to be more careful.

Jo <u>realy</u> <u>likd</u> to write and she started selling her stories to the <u>newspapper</u>.

really liked
newspaper

But one of her <u>frends didnt</u> like that kind of story so she <u>stoped</u> signing her name.

friends didn't
stopped

Don't you have any thoughts about your own life to add?

Document 3

A conversation with Kenny

Ms. Riley: Kenny, in my grade book I noticed I don't have a check for your literature logs. But I'm sure you've been reading, since I've seen you read at least two books a week since the beginning of the year.

Kenny: Yeah, I read three books last week.

Ms. Riley: I noticed how much you enjoyed one of them, at least—you were laughing as you read during silent reading. Did you choose one you wanted to write about in your literature log?

Kenny: Well, right now I'm reading an interesting one that takes place in a museum.

Ms. Riley: Oh, what book is that?

Kenny: It's a long name, *From the Mixed-Up Files of Mrs. Basil E. Frankenweiler.* I just started it last night.

Ms. Riley: Oh, I know that book. It's very good.

Kenny: Great, because I have a question about it.

Ms. Riley: Is it a question that could help with your reading?

Kenny: Well someone keeps explaining things to Saxonberg and I don't know who is explaining. I don't know who Saxonberg is either.

Ms. Riley: You know, Kenny, I think if you read a few more chapters you will probably find out, and then you can write about it in your lit log.

Kenny: Well, I can tell you about it tomorrow. It has a long name, but it's a small book. I'll finish it tonight.

Ms. Riley: Well, I'd really love to see it written in your lit log or I won't be able to fill in that you've completed your homework.

Kenny: That's O.K.—I don't read to get credit. I just read for fun.

Here is the first question related to the "Ms. Riley" case.

Question 1

1. **Review Document 1, the Literature Log Project Plan. The plan demonstrates both strengths and weaknesses.**

   - **Identify ONE strength and ONE weakness of the Literature Log Project Plan.**

   - **Describe how each strength or weakness you identified demonstrates a strength or weakness in planning instruction. Base your response on principles of effective instructional planning.**

Think about what is being asked.

In the space below, state in your own words what you think the question is asking.

Compare your impression of what is being asked with the explanation below.

The question asks for

   - *one* strength of the plan and *one* weakness of the plan

   - explanations of why *each* is a strength or a weakness

Think about the categories being assessed.

   - Planning instruction

As you saw in studying the questions and domains for the first case presented, planning instruction is a very important category and is addressed in many of the questions in the cases. Planning instruction draws on an understanding of learning theory, subject matter, curriculum development, and student development and a sense of how to use that knowledge in planning instruction.

In the *Principles of Learning and Teaching* test, rather than being asked to plan a unit or lesson plan of your own, you are asked to analyze existing plans in terms of strengths and weaknesses or in terms of how to modify them for specific purposes.

Write your response.

In the space below, write what you consider to be a response that directly addresses the question.

Reflect on your response in light of the scoring guide, sample responses, and commentary.

Now consider your response in light of the following scoring guide used to evaluate test-takers' responses. Remember that the guide contains illustrative possible responses that are neither restrictive nor prescriptive.

Scoring Guide for Question 1

Score of 2

The response presents one appropriate strength of the plan and one appropriate weakness of the plan and explains why each is a strength or a weakness. Here are some examples:

Strengths:

- Having students read independently for over two hours a week is likely to help them improve their reading skills.

- Letting each student choose the books to read reinforces the notion that individual differences are worth respecting.

- Writing four entries a week gives each student a significant amount of writing practice and can improve each student's writing fluency.

- The assignment to include a summary of the part of the book just read supports the objective of having students write accurate summaries.

- Having students link events in their lives to events in what they read directly supports the first objective.

- Having each student indicate what will happen next can build a student's critical thinking ability.

- Focusing on the dilemmas the characters face and how the reader would solve them promotes critical thinking and acknowledgment of individual differences.

Weaknesses:

- Assessing the number of pages read each week does not necessarily support any of the long-term goals or the objectives. It is, therefore, an inappropriate criterion for assessment.

- Keeping track of the number of entries in the log each week suggests that the teacher really wants more than the four entries she requires. Although having the students read more each week supports the goal of building reading skills, it does not necessarily promote the joy of reading suggested by the caps in the assignment: HAPPY READING.

- There is no aspect of the project assignment or the assessment that addresses the long-term goal of building a positive classroom community.

- The assessment does not match the goals and objectives, with the exception of the assessment of writing effective summaries. The assessment does not address critical thinking skills, individual differences, building a positive classroom community, or using writing to link reading and personal experience.

Score of 1

The response offers one appropriate strength or one appropriate weakness and appropriate reasons why it is a strength or weakness, such as those presented in score point 2, or one strength and one weakness without appropriate reasons why each is a strength or a weakness.

Score of 0

The response fails to address the question, presents inappropriate strengths and weaknesses, or is vague.

Response that would receive a score of 2.

Ms. Riley's goals and assignment are fairly well matched. She assigns a reasonable amount of reading for a week to address the goal of improving reading, attempts to help the students make personal connections to their lives, allows them to select their own books, and asks them to write regularly about what they read. Generally, her assignment develops her goals pretty well. However, her assessments are not well aligned with her goals. All of her assessments focus on mechanical aspects of the tasks she assigns. By grading student summaries and the number of entries, and counting the number of pages, she is suggesting that she is not very interested in critical thinking or in helping students to acknowledge differences among people. She establishes these as her goals, but when it comes to assessing student performance in the project, most of the goals and objectives do not count toward a grade, and therefore they are undervalued.

Commentary on the above response

The response presents both one appropriate strength and one appropriate weakness. The response is very fully developed; however, responses are evaluated on the appropriateness and/or accuracy of the information presented, not on the writing skill with which they are presented. The response receives full credit because it explains one appropriate strength and one appropriate weakness. Note that had the strength and weakness simply been named, without an explanation of why each was selected, the response would have received a score of 1.

Response that would receive a score of 1.

Having the students include a summary of the part of the book just read supports one of the objectives, the one that says students should write accurate summaries. In addition, having students link events in their lives to events in the books helps students see connections between their lives and what occurs in literature, and so matches another of the objectives.

Commentary on the above response

The response presents two appropriate strengths of the assignment. However, the question calls for one strength and one weakness. It therefore receives partial credit.

Response that would receive a score of 0.

I think having students keep literature logs is a very good idea. It helps them to think about what they have read, and gives them a chance to use their writing skills to write about something they know. A second good thing about these logs is that they give the teacher a way to assess what students have understood and are thinking.

Commentary on the above response

The response does not address the question. While a different question might have asked for advantages of this kind of assignment, the question as presented asks for one strength and one weakness of this specific plan. It therefore receives no credit.

Here is the second question related to the "Ms. Riley" case.

Question 2

2. Review Sharon's first entry (dated October 13) in Document 2, her literature log. Suppose that Ms. Riley wants to evaluate how well the entry demonstrates achievement of her long-term goals and/or her objectives.

    - Identify TWO aspects of Sharon's October 13 entry in her literature log that an effective evaluation would identify as achieving of one or more of Ms. Riley's goals and/or her objectives.

    - For each aspect you identified, explain how it demonstrates achievement of one or more of Ms. Riley's goals and/or her objectives. Base your response on principles of effective assessment and evaluation.

Think about what is being asked.

In the space below, state in your own words what you think the question is asking.

Compare your impression of what is being asked with the explanation below.

The question asks for

- *two* aspects of the first entry that show achievement of *one or more* of Ms. Riley's long-term goals and/or her objectives

- for *each* aspect, an explanation of how it meets one or more of the goals and/or objectives

Think about the categories being assessed.

- Assessment (diagnostic and evaluative)

An important aspect of this category is the ability to use formal and informal assessment strategies to evaluate the continuous intellectual development of the learner. This question asks for an assessment of Sharon's work and of Ms. Riley's ability to assess and respond to that work effectively.

Write your response.

In the space below, write what you consider to be a response that directly addresses the question.

Reflect on your response in light of the scoring guide, sample responses, and commentary.

Scoring Guide for Question 2

Score of 2

The response identifies and explains two appropriate achievements of one or more instructional goals or objectives, such as the following:

- Sharon notes that characters miss hearing Beth humming. She figures out from this that Beth is dead. She is using her critical thinking skills to figure out what is happening in the text.

- By including her mother's definition of "yufamisms" Sharon is connecting what happens in the book to her family, thereby making direct links between literature and her life.

- Sharon is writing an accurate summary of what happens in the book.

- By wondering what it is like to die, Sharon is indicating her own individuality and trying to wrestle with one of the dilemmas both she and the characters face.

- Sharon's entry is quite candid and unique, expressing her own unique point of view.

- Sharon trusts Ms. Riley to respect individual differences by "confessing" a great deal about her own private questions, family events, and dilemmas about the sensitive subject of death.

Score of 1

The response identifies and explains one appropriate achievement of one or more instructional goals or objectives, such as those presented in score point 2, or identifies but does not explain two aspects of the literature log entry that achieve one or more instructional goal or objective.

Score of 0

The response fails to address the question, presents inappropriate achievements, or is vague.

Response that would receive a score of 2.

Sharon is a sensitive, thoughtful reader who in her first response offers Ms. Riley many of the things Ms. Riley wants to promote in readers. She talks about her own personal links to the characters when she discusses the death of Beth and her aunt, uses her analytic powers to figure out the meaning of dilemmas that characters face when she uses clues to figure out that Beth has died, and suggests how personally she responds to key events in the novel when she notes that she wonders what it felt like to die.

Commentary on the above response

The response presents and explains at least two appropriate ways in which Sharon's entry demonstrates achievement of the objectives. Adding a third appropriate way neither adds to nor subtracts from the effectiveness of the response. It receives full credit.

Response that would receive a score of 1.

In the first entry, Sharon does a wonderful job of connecting what she has read to her own life. When she talks about one of the characters dying, and then connects that to her aunt's death, she has done a wonderful job of making a connection. She has really met her teacher's objective!

Commentary on the above response

The response presents and explains only one appropriate way in which Sharon's first entry demonstrates achievement of one or more of the objectives. It therefore receives partial credit.

Response that would receive a score of 0.

Sharon's first entry is wonderful! I wish I could get my students to write reading log entries like this one. She does everything her teacher wanted, and more! I just wish Ms. Riley had given her a lot more positive feedback.

Commentary on the above response

The response does talk about the first entry, but it does not address the question, which asks for specific ways in which the entry demonstrates achievement of one or more of the objectives. It receives no credit.

Here is the third question related to the "Ms. Riley" case.

Question 3

3. **In Document 2, Sharon's literature log, there are significant differences between Sharon's entry dated October 13 and her entry dated October 27. It appears that Sharon is having less success meeting the objectives for the project in the October 27 entry than in the October 13 entry.**

    ■ **Identify TWO significant differences between the first and second entries that indicate that Sharon is having less success in meeting the objectives of the project in the second entry.**

    ■ **For each difference you identified, suggest how Ms. Riley might have responded differently to Sharon in order to help Sharon continue to meet the objectives of the project. Base your response on principles of communication, assessment, and/or effective instruction.**

Think about what is being asked.

In the space below, state in your own words what you think the question is asking.

Compare your impression of what is being asked with the explanation below.

The question asks for

■ *two* specific differences between the first entry and the second

■ for *each* difference, how Ms. Riley might have helped Sharon continue to meet her goals

Think about the categories being assessed.

■ Planning instruction

■ Communication, social organization, classroom management

■ Assessment

The question addresses all three of these important domains in one way or another. Part of planning instruction is using an understanding of student development. Communication addresses using knowledge of effective verbal communication techniques to foster active inquiry, while assessment involves formal and informal assessment strategies to evaluate the continuous intellectual development of the learner. The ways in which Ms. Riley thinks about her responses as she plans, the way in which she assesses the achievement of her objectives, and the way in which she communicates with Sharon all directly address these domains.

Write your response.

In the space below, write what you consider to be a response that directly addresses the question.

Reflect on your response in light of the scoring guide, sample responses, and commentary.

Scoring Guide for Question 3

Score of 2

The response presents two significant differences between Sharon's October 13 and October 27 entries and offers appropriate suggestions about how Ms. Riley could have helped Sharon to meet the teacher's goals, such as the following:

- As Ms. Riley requested, Sharon's second entry summarizes what happened in the book, but doesn't discuss any of the dilemmas the characters face. Because Ms. Riley doesn't comment on the dilemma Sharon included in the first entry, Sharon probably believes that is not important. Had she praised Sharon for including her remarks on the dilemmas faced in the first entry, Sharon might have included dilemmas in the second entry.

- Sharon's first entry draws connections to the student's life with her reference to her mother's definition and to her aunt's death. Had Ms. Riley noted how interesting those comments were, Sharon might have included similar comments in the second entry.

- Sharon's first entry engages in introspective speculation when she comments, "I wonder what it felt like." This is a kind of thinking skill Ms. Riley suggests she wants to develop. Had she commented positively about it, Sharon would have been more likely to continue doing this kind of thinking.

- The second entry is a minimal summary and does not give any evidence of Sharon's using critical thinking skills, such as her ability to figure out Beth's death in the first entry. Had Ms. Riley praised Sharon's ability to think critically to figure out that Beth had died, Sharon would have been more likely to continue using this critical thinking skill.

- By focusing her comments in response to the October 13 entry largely on matters of routine requirements (title, author, pages read) and on spelling, with only a two-word comment on a personal response, Ms. Riley implies that the routine requirements are much more important than the ability to write an accurate summary or to link aspects of the text with experiences and people in their own lives. Had she focused on the summary and the connections, Sharon would have been more likely to continue developing the skills to address these aspects of the assignment.

Score of 1

The response presents one significant difference between the October 13 and the October 27 entries and offers one appropriate way in which Ms. Riley could help Sharon to meet the teacher's goals, such as those presented in score point 2, or the response presents two significant differences between the October 13 and the October 27 entries with no ways in which Ms. Riley could have responded differently to Sharon.

Score of 0

The response fails to address the question, presents inappropriate differences, or is vague.

Response that would receive a score of 2.

In Sharon's second entry, the student includes the kinds of things Ms. Riley says she wants to see when she comments on Sharon's first entry. She gives title and author and pages read, and does include a very short summary. However, she omits any personal connections to the literature or focusing on any dilemmas the characters face because Ms. Riley makes no comment on those aspects of Sharon's first entry. If Ms. Riley had sympathized with Sharon when she gave Ms. Riley what she asked for or praised her for including some of the aspects the teacher requested, Sharon might have included them in the second entry.

Commentary on the above response

The response presents two appropriate and significant differences (the second entry does include all the specific information the teacher says she wants about title, author, and pages read but omits any personal connections to literature or discussion of dilemmas the characters face). It also presents appropriate suggestions for how Ms. Riley might have responded in a way that would have helped Sharon meet the goals. The response receives full credit.

Response would receive a score of 1.

One significant difference is that Sharon stopped sharing ways that the book reminded her of her own life. If Ms. Riley had commented favorably and constructively on the connections Sharon made in the first entry, Sharon might have continued working in this way to achieve the objective. The second difference is that the first entry is a lot longer. If Ms. Riley had praised her for writing a lot, she might have continued developing her fluency in this way.

Commentary on the above response

The response presents one appropriate difference, but then discusses a difference that does not indicate that Sharon is having less success meeting the objectives for the project. The response therefore receives partial credit.

Response that would receive a score of 0.

Ms. Riley is really missing an opportunity to help Sharon. Students this age are very sensitive and I suspect Sharon had a pretty negative reaction when she got her literature log back after the first entry. Ms. Riley could profit from a professional development workshop that helps teachers develop effective ways to respond to student logs.

Commentary on the above response

The response, while it makes some valid points, does not address the question which requires an identification of significant differences between the two entries and ways Ms. Riley might help Sharon continue to meet her goals. It therefore receives no credit.

Here is the fourth question related to the "Ms. Riley" case.

Question 4

4. In Document 3, Kenny's conversation with Ms. Riley, Kenny reveals characteristics of himself as a learner that could be used to support his development of literacy skills.

    ■ Identify ONE characteristic of Kenny as a learner and then suggest ONE strategy Ms. Riley might use to address that characteristic in a way that will support his development of literacy skills.

    ■ Describe how the strategy you suggested addresses the characteristic of Kenny as a learner and how the strategy could support Kenny's development of literacy skills. Base your response on principles of varied instructional strategies for different learners and of human development.

Think about what is being asked.

In the space below, state in your own words what you think the question is asking.

Compare your impression of what is being asked with the explanation below.

The question asks for

■ *one* characteristic of Kenny as a learner and *one* strategy Ms. Riley might use to address that characteristic to support his development of literacy skills

■ descriptions of how the strategy addresses the characteristics of Kenny as a learner and supports development of his literacy skill

Think about what is being assessed.

■ Human development

■ Varied instructional strategies for different kinds of learners

These two domains are both very important in understanding students and their needs and planning instruction to meet those needs. Both are directly involved in understanding Kenny and his needs as a learner, and planning strategies to meet his specific needs.

Write your response.

In the space below, write what you consider to be a response that directly addresses the question.

Reflect on your response in light of the scoring guide, sample responses, and commentary.

Scoring Guide for Question 4

Score of 2

The response identifies and describes one appropriate characteristic of Kenny as a learner and one appropriate strategy Ms. Riley can use to address that characteristic and support the development of Kenny's literacy skills.

- Kenny loves to read, but doesn't want to take the time to write about what he's read. Ms. Riley might make the writing more creative to match Kenny's interest in books. She could ask Kenny to think about what makes a book interesting to him, thereby supporting his critical thinking, or might provide an alternate mode, such as a tape-recording, for Kenny to record his thoughts.

- Ms. Riley might ask Kenny to imitate the plot of a book he likes in order to create his own story. That would link Kenny's love of reading with writing that would indicate what Kenny takes from the books he reads.

- Ms. Riley might ask Kenny to write a review of one of the books he likes so that others in the class will want to read it. That links Kenny's writing to a purpose supported by his inherent interest in books.

- Ms. Riley might give Kenny some reviews or analysis of the books he's read and ask him to analyze whether or not the reviews or analysis are accurate from his perspective. That will give Kenny insights into the act of reviewing as well as reading books.

- Because Kenny is intrigued by books, Ms. Riley might ask Kenny to select a small group and act out a scene from one of his favorite books. That will allow Kenny to develop a more critical perspective on a book he's reading.

- Ms. Riley might ask Kenny to search the Internet for articles about an author Kenny admires. She might then have him analyze the book from the perspective of the author. This activity might spark Kenny's interest in the connections between an author's life and some of the characters in his/her books.

Score of 1

The response identifies and describes one appropriate characteristic of Kenny as a learner such as those presented in score point 2, but does not present a strategy Ms. Riley can use to address that characteristic and support the development of Kenny's literacy skills, or identifies an appropriate characteristic of Kenny as a learner and a strategy Ms. Riley could use to address that characteristic, but does not sufficiently describe either the characteristic or the strategy.

Score of 0

The response fails to address the question, presents inappropriate identification of characteristics of Kenny as a learner and strategies to address those characteristics, or is vague.

Response that would receive a score of 2

Because Kenny is an avid reader, Ms. Riley needs to think of a strategy that might engage Kenny in critical thinking that can enhance his literacy. Since one of her long-term goals includes developing speaking abilities, she might offer him the opportunity to tape-record his comments about the book, moving the apparent focus from writing to talking about the book—something it appears he likes to do. To address her goal of developing critical thinking skills, she might give him a few analyses of books by reviewers and ask Kenny to support or refute the reviews from his reading of the book.

Commentary on the above response

The response begins by identifying an appropriate characteristic of Kenny as a learner, and then presents and describes an appropriate strategy Ms. Riley might use to address that characteristic in a way that would address her first long-term goal. The response receives full credit, Score Point 2.

Response that would receive a score of 1.

Kenny is a very interesting learner. He obviously loves to read; Ms. Riley comments she's seen him read at least two books a week, and he himself says he just reads "for fun." But he candidly admits he doesn't "read to get credit," and so he isn't concerned about the assignment Ms. Riley has given, nor about meeting her objectives. Students like Kenny are a challenge: he loves reading (good for him!) but doesn't want to jump through Ms. Riley's hoops. She has to be creative to figure out how to challenge him!

Commentary on the above response

The response analyzes Kenny as a learner with appropriate commentary. However, simply saying that Ms. Riley "has to be creative to figure out how to challenge him" is not sufficient to meet the second requirement of the question. The response therefore receives partial credit.

Response that would receive a score of 0.

There isn't really enough information given here to do an analysis of Kenny as a learner, nor to suggest how his teacher could work to support his development of literacy skills. A much fuller presentation of his work, his thoughts, and his interactions with his teacher and the other students would be needed.

Commentary on the above response

As was pointed out earlier, saying that "more information is needed" is not an acceptable response nor a viable excuse for not responding to the question. While it is true that more information could and would be sought to do a full analysis of Kenny or a complete plan for addressing his needs, there is sufficient information in the short conversation presented to warrant "one characteristic of Kenny as a learner" and one strategy to address that characteristic.

Here is the fifth question related to the "Ms. Riley" case.

Question 5

5. **Review Ms. Riley's long-term goals at the beginning of Document 1, the Literature Log Project Plan.**

   ■ **Select TWO long-term goals, and for each goal, identify one strategy Ms. Riley might use to expand the literature log unit beyond the stated assignment and assessment plan to address the goal.**

   ■ **Explain how the use of each strategy you identified could expand the literature log unit to address the selected goal. Base your response on principles of planning instruction and/or language development and acquisition.**

Think about what is being asked.

In the space below, state in your own words what you think the question is asking.

Compare your impression of what is being asked with the explanation below.

The question asks for

   ■ *two* goals

   ■ for *each* goal, explanation of one strategy to expand the literature log

Think about the categories being assessed.

- Planning instruction

- Language development and acquisition

Both planning instruction and planning strategies to support the language learning of all students are important skills. The literature log is a part of Ms. Riley's literacy program; by asking you to plan strategies she might use to expand the literature log assignment, the question directly assesses both categories.

Write your response.

In the space below, write what you consider to be a response that directly addresses the question.

Reflect on your response in light of the scoring guide, sample responses, and commentary.

Scoring Guide for Question 5

Score of 2

The response selects two long-term goals and identifies an appropriate strategy to address each goal with explanations of how the use of each strategy could address the selected goal, such as the following:

- One goal is to develop speaking and listening abilities. To develop these skills, Ms. Riley can include activities such as having students report aloud about the books read while other students note what is important about each and ask questions about the books.

- One goal is to develop critical thinking skills. Ms. Riley could have included in her assessment plan a rubric that would provide a means for student self-assessment and for her own assessment of the kinds of critical thinking skills she has included in the assignment.

- One goal is to build a positive classroom community, but this goal is never addressed. Ms. Riley might form cooperative groups based on principles of teaching social skills and have the groups read members' literature logs, identifying positive ways to see the differences in how members of the group responded to what they read.

- One goal is to address students' individual differences. Ms. Riley could read all the logs and find significant differences among the ways students responded. She could then present those examples to the class and conduct a class discussion about how interesting and valuable those differences are.

- To address the goal of linking aspects of a text with experiences and people in their own lives, Ms. Riley could use an overhead projector to display features of the logs that presented intriguing ways in which individuals made connections between what they read and their own lives. In this case, she should check first with students to be sure she has not invaded their privacy. The class could discuss those connections and offer further suggestions about how individual class members might respond.

- To address the goal of improving reading, writing, speaking and listening, Ms. Riley can have each student maintain a folder of literature log entries for several weeks and then select two for public presentation. The student could then rewrite each entry to present to the class in published form. This adds audience and purpose to the assignment.

- To address the goal of improving speaking and listening skills, Ms. Riley can form groups and have students present an oral summary of their book and why it was important to them. They can also explain to their group why others might want to read the book as well. Each group could then select one or two for presentation to the whole class. The activity could develop speaking and listening skills and generate more interest in books that students might want to read.

- To address the goal of building a positive classroom community, Ms. Riley can form groups of those who have read the same or similar books. She could then have the members of the group explain some of the individual connections they made to what happened in the book, or comment about one or two things each finds interesting about each student's response to the characters. By sharing responses to books, students build a sense of a community.

- To address the goal of building critical thinking skills, Ms. Riley can ask students who identified interesting dilemmas in books to explain what was problematic for the characters and why. Ms. Riley could use these dilemmas to begin a class discussion about human dilemmas all people face.

- To address her long-term goal of building a positive classroom community and her objectives of both linking reading to experience and developing summary writing skills, Ms. Riley can form response groups in which students share their logs. She could establish the principle that there are to be no "put downs," and that students must find one or two positive things to say about the connections others draw to the texts or about the summaries.

Score of 1

The response selects two long-term goals and, for each, identifies but does not explain an appropriate strategy to address the goal, such as those presented in score point 2, or selects one long-term goal and identifies and explains an appropriate strategy to address the goal.

Score of 0

The response fails to address the question, presents inappropriate goals and strategies, or is vague.

Response that would receive a score of 2.

Ms. Riley has many valuable long-term goals that could be developed through additional activities or assessments. For example, one of her goals is to build a positive classroom community. To address this goal, she could create cooperative groups and have students respond in positive ways to the connections other students have made between their books and their own lives or to the summaries that are written. If several students have read the same book, she could have them share their summaries and personal responses, developing a sense of the commonality of their reading and personal experiences. Another of her goals is to address students' individual differences. After checking with students to be sure they are comfortable with sharing, she might discuss or present on an overhead projector a variety of kinds of connections students make between books and their own lives, to show how each reader responds in ways that are unique.

Commentary on the above response

The response presents two goals and fully discusses an appropriate strategy Ms. Riley might use to expand the literature log to implement the goal. The response fully and appropriately addresses the question and receives full credit.

Response that would receive a score of 1.

One of her goals is to build critical thinking skills. To address this goal, Ms. Riley can ask students who came up with some interesting dilemmas in books to explain what was difficult for the characters and to tell why they thought the situation was difficult. Ms. Riley could use these dilemmas to start a class discussion about problems all people face. In this way, she would be addressing one of her important goals and at the same time extending the lesson.

Commentary on the above response

The response only partially addresses the requirements of the question. The question calls for an identification of "two goals" and one strategy for each that can be used to expand the literature log unit. The response identifies only one goal and does present a strategy to address it in a way that would expand the unit. The response receives partial credit.

Response that would receive a score of 0.

I don't think it would really be a good idea to try to expand the literature log unit at this time. Third-grade teachers have an enormous amount of material to cover. For each subject, there are state, district, and school standards of objectives to meet. If she adds to this unit, she is going to be taking away time and emphasis from other subjects like social studies, mathematics, or science. All of these need a lot of instructional time. I think she should leave well enough alone.

Commentary on the above response

Arguing with the question is not an acceptable way to respond. While the points made in the response may be seen as having some validity, it must be assumed that Ms. Riley could expand the unit within the time she has for her language arts program. Because the response does not address the question, it receives no credit.

Here is the sixth question related to the "Ms. Riley" case.

Question 6

6. **Review the two objectives of the Literature Log Project Plan included in Document 1. Suppose that at the end of the project, as a culminating activity, Ms. Riley wants her students to use their literature logs to help them do a self-assessment of the two objectives.**

   - **For each of the TWO project objectives described in Document 1, suggest one assignment Ms. Riley could give the students that would serve as a self-assessment.**

   - **For each assignment you suggested, describe how Ms. Riley's students could use it as a self-assessment. Base your response on principles of effective assessment.**

Think about what is being asked.

In the space below, state in your own words what you think the question is asking.

Compare your impression of what is being asked with the explanation below.

The question asks for two proposed assignments:

- *one* to serve as a self-assessment for students based on the *first* objective mentioned in Document 1

- *one* to serve as a self-assessment for students based on the *second* objective mentioned in Document 1

Think about the categories being evaluated.

- Assessment

Part of the assessment domain involves teaching students how to assess their own work. Self-assessment can help students make connections between learning objectives and their own performance.

Write your response.

In the space below, write what you consider to be a response that directly addresses the question.

Reflect on your response in light of the scoring guide, sample responses, and commentary.

Scoring Guide for Question 6

Score of 2

The response presents an explanation of two appropriate culminating activities: one that will help students do a self-assessment of the first objective, and one that will help students do a self-assessment of the second objective, such as the following:

Objective #1

- She could have them select three entries that they believe meet the objective of linking aspects of their reading with experiences and people in their own lives. For each entry, explain why it meets the objective.

- She could have them write a new paragraph about a character or event that they felt strongly connected to, and explain why.

- She could have them select one entry that they feel they could improve in terms of making connections to their own lives and write a revision and one entry that they feel meets the objective and tell why.

- She could have the class develop a rubric for evaluating entries in terms of making connections between reading and personal experience, and use the rubric to evaluate selected entries.

Objective #2

- She could have the class develop a rubric for an effective summary and have individuals use it to evaluate three of their own entries.

- She could have each student read five or six of their summaries and write a reflective assessment about the strengths or weaknesses they see in the summaries.

- She could have the class write a summary of a short selection they all read and use a class-developed rubric to have them evaluate their own summaries.

Score of 1

The response presents an explanation of one appropriate culminating activity that will help students do a self-assessment of either the first objective or the second objective, such as those presented in score point 2, or the response suggests two culminating activities related to the objectives but does not describe how the students could use them as self-assessments.

Score of 0

The response fails to address the question, presents inappropriate culminating activities, or is vague.

Response that would receive a score of 2.

For both objectives, her activity for the students to do self-assessment could begin with the development of a rubric for evaluating success in meeting the objective. Students could work together to develop both rubrics. Then, for the first objective, she could have students select three of their own entries and use the rubric to evaluate how well each student met the objective. For the second objective, Ms. Riley could have the students write a summary of a new selection, and then use the rubric to evaluate how well they have learned to write an effective summary.

Commentary on the above response

The response presents one appropriate assignment for each objective. Although the response begins by explaining something that both activities could have in common, it includes separate appropriate activities for each of the two objectives. It receives full credit.

Response that would receive a score of 1.

Following up with a culminating self-assessment is a very good way to end the project. It will help students internalize what they have learned. There are many different activities she could use. One is that she could have them select one entry that they feel could be improved in terms of making connections to their own lives. They would then write a revision and one entry that they feel meets the objective and tell why. Doing these two things would really help them take a fresh look at what it means to connect literature to their own lives.

Commentary on the above response

The response suggests that there are two activities, but they address only one of the objectives. The question specifically calls for one activity for each of the two objectives. It therefore receives only partial credit.

Response that would receive a score of 0.

In a sense, it's a very good idea for her to do a culminating activity. But, on the other hand, it's very possible that by now the students have learned everything there is to learn about writing literature logs. They have been doing it for several months, and I have found that students of this age get tired of activities after a while. I would therefore suggest that she just wrap up the literature logs with a celebration in which she praises them for what they have done well, and then move on to some other aspect of literature study.

Commentary on the above response

The response begins with what appears to be a direct response to the question, but moves off the point and fails to address the question, instead arguing with its premise. Responses that argue with the question are deemed non-responsive and receive no credit.

This chapter was designed to give you a good idea of how the constructed-response sections of the test are scored and to offer you advice and opportunities for practice. You have been guided step-by-step through twelve practice questions and have been shown evaluations of sample responses at each score level. We suggest that you now apply the knowledge and skills gained in this chapter to a practice test containing two new case studies and twelve questions, which can be found in chapter 6.

Chapter 6

Practice Test—Case Studies with
Constructed-Response Questions

► ► ► ► ► ► ► ► ► ► ► ►

Now that you have studied the content topics and have worked through strategies relating to reading case studies and answering constructed-response questions, you should take the following practice test. You will probably find it helpful to simulate actual testing conditions. Find a quiet place where you will not be interrupted for at least one hour.

Set a timer or an alarm for 70 minutes. (In the real testing situation, the test supervisor will mark the time for you and warn you when you have a few minutes left.)

When you have finished the practice test, you should read the scoring guides and sample responses with commentaries in chapter 7 and assess for yourself how your response might have been scored.

Professional Assessments for Beginning Teachers ®

TEST NAME:

Principles of Learning and Teaching

Practice Case Histories and Constructed-Response Questions

Time—70 minutes

12 Questions

CASE HISTORY I

(Questions 1–6)

Approximate time—35 Minutes

Mr. Jenner is a second-year teacher in a middle school with high test scores and high academic standards. In his English/History core class there are twenty-five heterogeneously mixed 12 and 13 year olds. He is beginning the fourth week of instruction.

Document 1

Project plan

World Cultures Panel Presentations

Objectives:

Students will

1. Review and use concepts about world cultures

2. Demonstrate speaking and listening skills

3. Use creativity (art, literature, music, multimedia, objects)

4. Use higher-order thinking skills

Assignment:

1. You will work in assigned groups of five

2. Each group will select one culture from a list

3. The group will plan, gather information, and present a panel report to the class on the culture

4. Use the characteristics of a culture studied last week to organize your presentation

5. Include some use of art, literature, music, multimedia, or other cultural objects

6. All students must participate in group planning and presentation

Activities:	Periods
1. Presentation/discussion of assignment; video of effective panel from another class; assign groups	1
2. Group work: select culture; plan presentation, assign responsibilities	1
3. Group work: prepare presentations	3
4. Panel presentations	5
5. Writing assignment: comparison/contrast of cultures	1

Assessment:

1. Group work: individual and group grade
2. Panel presentation: individual and group grade
3. Writing assignment

At Mr. Jenner's request, Mr. Rose, a core program supervisor, is observing and tape-recording the class in order to make suggestions for improvement.

Document 2

Supervisor's notes and transcript of tape Mr. Jenner's class after lunch

September 24

When the bell rings, about half the students are seated at their desks. Four students are standing at the door. Three others are tossing around an object in the back. Several others are walking around visiting. There is loud conversation.

Mr. Jenner: Class, attention please!

There is little or no response

Mr. Jenner: [louder] Attention!! Please get seated immediately! Get away from the door, Theo, Tom, Christi, and Julia. Sit down Jack, Huberto, and Kang.

Some scuffling near the classroom door; Christi and Julia slowly move toward their seats, laughing. Theo and Tom still at door. Three boys continue tossing the object.

Mr. Jenner: Please move into the cooperative groups I assigned yesterday for the panel reports.

Noise level rises again; students move desks noisily. Several students speak loudly at the same time.

Tom: Which group am I in?

Christi: Javier just took my backpack, Mr. Jenner. (She laughs) Come on, Javier—give it back. Mr. Jenner! Make him!

Elaine: Can we change groups, Mr. Jenner?

Kim: Something just hit me right in the head. I think I have a concussion. (Several students laugh)

Kia: I've lost my assignment sheet. What are we supposed to do?

Leroy: Hey! Who's the guy with the tape recorder?

Mr. Jenner: O.K., that's enough! You know what you're supposed to do. Begin your planning. Please start now!

Noise level dies down; some students begin work. Boys in the back continue throwing the object.

Mr. Jenner: Jack, Huberto, Kang: into your groups now.

Boys throw the object again. Several other students snicker.

Mr. Jenner: Okay, that's it. All three of you—to the office right now. I'm calling them to let them know you're coming.

Gradually the noise subsides; few groups function well. Confusion about assignments and responsibilities continues for the rest of the period.

Document 3

Conversation with a colleague

September 24

After school, Ms. Young, a colleague, pokes her head into Mr. Jenner's classroom.

Ms. Young: Hi. How'd it go when Mr. Rose came in today?

Mr. Jenner: To tell you the truth, things weren't so good.

Ms. Young: What happened?

Mr. Jenner: My class was totally out of control—and I'd really worked on the planning because Mr. Rose was coming in. But I don't think it's anything anyone can help me with....

Ms. Young: What do you mean?

Mr. Jenner: Well, to be honest I think I just got the worst of the lot. The principal told me they're "a typical range of kids this age," but I gotta tell you, I don't think these kids are typical.

Ms. Young: Don't be so sure. They may be more typical than you think.

Document 4

Mr. Jenner's class assignment

September 26

I want to get your ideas about a class problem. The behavior of most students is not what is expected here. Please tell me:

- What you think are the causes of the problem

- How the problem has affected you

- What solutions you think might work

Document 5

Two student responses

Tony's response

I think the problem is that when you give directions, some kids don't hear because others are talking. When they don't get in trouble, everyone thinks it's O.K. to continue fooling around. Why can't you give directions so everyone has to listen and some of us who want to can start?

Leroy's response

Hey, Mr. J—lighten up! It's no big deal. We're just kickin' back before we work. We're learning stuff—go with the flow! Ask the guy with the tape recorder—he'll tell you we're good kids. Just give us a break.

Questions 1–6 require you to write short answers. Base your answers on your knowledge of principles of learning and teaching. Be sure to answer all parts of the questions. Write your answers in the space indicated on the pages that follow.

1. Document 1, Mr. Jenner's project plan for World Cultures Panel Presentations, demonstrates several aspects of effective instructional planning.

   ■ Identify TWO strengths of Mr. Jenner's project plan.

   ■ Explain how each strength demonstrates an aspect of effective instructional planning. Base your response on principles of effective instructional planning.

2. Review the assessment section of Document 1, Mr. Jenner's project plan.

   ■ Suggest TWO ways in which Mr. Jenner could strengthen the assessment section of his project plan in order to provide students with a better opportunity to demonstrate their accomplishments on this project.

   ■ For each suggestion you made, describe how it would provide students a better opportunity to demonstrate their accomplishments on this project. Base your response on principles of formal and informal assessment.

3. Assume that Mr. Jenner and Mr. Rose discuss the beginning of the class that Mr. Rose observed, with the focus on the first few minutes when students enter the room, before they begin to move to cooperative groups.

   ■ Suggest TWO strategies Mr. Rose might recommend that Mr. Jenner use to make the transition from lunch to class smoother and less disruptive.

   ■ Explain how each strategy you suggested could improve the transition from lunch to class, making it smoother and less disruptive. Base your response on principles of classroom management.

4. Document 2, the transcript of the class and Mr. Rose's notations, indicates that Mr. Jenner could improve his use of cooperative groups.

   ■ Suggest TWO strategies that Mr. Rose might recommend that Mr. Jenner implement to make the cooperative groups work more effectively.

   ■ Explain how the use of each strategy you suggested could make the cooperative groups work more effectively. Base your response on principles of planning instruction and classroom management.

5. Review Document 3, Mr. Jenner's conversation with Ms. Young, in which he says the students in the class are "not typical" of students their age and she implies that perhaps they are.

   ■ Identify TWO individual or group behaviors described in Document 2 (the transcript of the class) and/or Document 5 (the student responses) that are typical of students ages 12 to 13.

   ■ For each behavior you identified, describe how it is typical of students ages 12 to 13. Base your response on principles of human development.

6. Assume that Mr. Jenner has read all of the student responses to the assignment on improving classroom behavior (Document 4).

   ■ Suggest TWO additional actions Mr. Jenner might take to further involve the class in improving classroom behavior.

   ■ For each action you suggested, explain how it is likely to be effective in improving classroom behavior. Base your response on principles of communication and classroom management.

Principles of Learning and Teaching

Write your response to Question 1 here.

_____

_____

_____

_____

_____

_____

_____

_____

_____

_____

_____

_____

_____

_____

_____

_____

_____

_____

_____

_____

Principles of Learning and Teaching

Write your response to Question 2 here.

_____

_____

_____

_____

_____

_____

_____

_____

_____

_____

_____

_____

_____

_____

_____

_____

_____

_____

_____

_____

_____

_____

Principles of Learning and Teaching

Write your response to Question 3 here.

_____

_____

_____

_____

_____

_____

_____

_____

_____

_____

_____

_____

_____

_____

_____

_____

_____

_____

_____

Principles of Learning and Teaching

Write your response to Question 4 here.

_____

_____

_____

_____

_____

_____

_____

_____

_____

_____

_____

_____

_____

_____

_____

_____

_____

_____

_____

_____

Principles of Learning and Teaching

Write your response to Question 5 here.

Principles of Learning and Teaching

Write your response to Question 6 here.

_____

_____

_____

_____

_____

_____

_____

_____

_____

_____

_____

_____

_____

_____

_____

_____

_____

_____

_____

_____

CASE HISTORY II

(Questions 7–12)

Approximate time—35 Minutes

Scenario

Mr. Payton teaches world history to a class of thirty heterogeneously grouped students ages 14 to 16. He is working with his supervisor, planning for his self-evaluation to be completed in the spring. At the beginning of the third week of school, he begins gathering material that might be helpful for the self-evaluation. He has selected one class and three students from this class to focus on.

Mr. Payton's first impression of the three students

Jimmy has attended school in the district for ten years. He repeated fifth and seventh grades. Two years older than most of the other students in class and having failed twice, Jimmy is neither dejected nor hostile. He is an outgoing boy who, on the first day of class, offered to help me with "the young kids" in the class. He said, "Don't worry about me remembering a lot of dates and stuff. I know it's going to be hard, and I'll probably flunk again anyway, so don't spend your time thinking about me."

Burns is a highly motivated student who comes from a family of world travelers. He has been to Europe and Asia. These experiences have influenced his career choice, international law. He appears quiet and serious. He has done extremely well on written assignments and appears to prefer to work alone or with one or two equally bright, motivated students. He has a childhood friend, one of the slowest students in the class.

Pauline is a withdrawn student whose grades for the previous two years have been mostly C's and D's. Although Pauline displays no behavior problems when left alone, she appears not to be popular with the other students. She often stares out the window when she should be working. When I speak to Pauline about completing assignments, she becomes hostile. She has completed few of the assignments so far with any success. When I spoke to her counselor, Pauline yelled at me, "Now I'm in trouble with my counselor too, all because you couldn't keep your mouth shut!"

Mr. Payton's initial self-analysis written for his supervisor

I attend workshops whenever I can and consider myself a creative teacher. I often divide the students into groups for cooperative projects, but they fall apart and are far from "cooperative." The better-performing students, like Burns, complain about the groups, claiming that small-group work is boring and that they learn more working alone or with students like themselves. I try to stimulate all the students' interest through class discussions. In these discussions, the high-achieving students seem more interested in impressing me than in listening and responding to what other students have to say. The low-achieving students seem content to be silent. Although I try most of the strategies I learn in workshops, I usually find myself returning to a modified lecture and the textbook as my instructional mainstays.

Background information on lesson to be observed by supervisor

Goals:

- To introduce students to important facts and theories about Catherine the Great

- To link students' textbook reading to other sources of information

- To give students practice in combining information from written and oral material

- To give students experience in note-taking

I assigned a chapter on Catherine the Great in the textbook as homework on Tuesday. Students are to take notes on their reading. I gave Jimmy a book on Catherine the Great with a narrative treatment rather than the factual approach taken by the textbook. I told him the only important date is the date Catherine began her reign. The book has more pictures and somewhat larger print than the textbook.

I made no adaptation for Burns, since he's doing fine. I offered to create a study guide for Pauline, but she angrily said not to bother. I hope that Wednesday's lecture will make up for any difficulties she might experience in reading the textbook.

Supervisor's notes on Wednesday's lesson

Mr. Payton gives a lecture on Catherine the Great. First he says, "It is important that you take careful notes because I will be including information that is not contained in the chapter you read as homework last night. The test I will give on Friday will include both the lecture and the textbook information." He tape records the lecture to supplement Pauline's notes, but does not tell Pauline about the tape until the period is over because he wants her to do the best note-taking she can manage. During the lecture, he speaks slowly, watching the class as they take notes. In addition, he walks about the classroom and glances at the students' notes.

Mr. Payton's follow-up and reflection

Tomorrow the students will use the class period to study for the test. I will offer Pauline earphones to listen to the tape-recorded lecture. On Friday, we will have a short-answer and essay test covering the week's work.

Class notes seem incomplete and inaccurate, and I'm not satisfied with this test as an assessment of student performance. Is that a fair measure of all they do?

Questions 7–12 require you to write short answers. Base your answers on your knowledge of principles of learning and teaching. Be sure to answer all parts of the questions. Write your answers in the spaces indicated on the pages that follow.

7. In his self-analysis, Mr. Payton says that the better-performing students say small-group work is boring and that they learn more working alone or only with students like themselves. Assume Mr. Payton wants to continue using cooperative learning groups because he believes they have value for all students.

   ■ Identify TWO strategies Mr. Payton could use to address the concerns of the students who complained and to make cooperative group work more effective.

   ■ For each strategy you identified, explain how its use could address the concerns of the students who complained and could make group work more effective. Base your response on principles of effective instructional strategies.

8. Review the section "Background information on lesson to be observed by supervisor," in which Mr. Payton describes the modifications he made to the lesson for Jimmy and Burns.

   ■ Suggest TWO other modifications, one for Jimmy and one for Burns, that Mr. Payton could have made that would have offered the students a better learning situation.

   ■ For each modification you suggested, explain how the modification could have provided Jimmy or Burns a better learning situation. Base your response on principles of varied instruction for diverse learners.

9. Mr. Payton's second and third goals are "To link students' textbook reading to other sources of information" and "To give students practice in combining information from written and oral material."

   ■ Suggest TWO strategies and/or activities Mr. Payton could use to help his students work toward meeting one or both of these goals.

   ■ For each strategy or activity you suggested, explain how its use could help students work toward meeting Mr. Payton's second and/or third goal(s). Base your response on principles of effective instructional planning and strategies.

10. Mr. Payton's fourth goal is "To give students experience in note-taking." Review the description of Wednesday's lesson and Mr. Payton's reflection on the lesson.

   ■ Suggest TWO additional strategies Mr. Payton could have used during the lecture to help all students take notes in a way that would support them as learners.

   ■ For each strategy you suggested, explain how its use could help all students take notes in a way that would support them as learners. Base your response on principles of effective instruction.

11. Mr. Payton comments in his reflection that he is not satisfied with just a test as a "fair measure of all they do."

   ■ Suggest TWO additional informal or formal assessment techniques Mr. Payton could use to provide his students with opportunities to demonstrate their learning.

   ■ For each technique you suggested, describe the kind(s) of information about student learning it could provide. Base your response on principles of informal and formal assessment.

12. Assume that Mr. Payton tells Pauline's counselor that he feels they need to learn more about Pauline as a learner so he can help her more effectively.

   ■ Describe TWO aspects of Pauline's behavior that Mr. Payton and Pauline's counselor might discuss in order to understand Pauline better as a learner.

   ■ For each aspect you described, suggest one hypothesis they might investigate to understand Pauline better as a learner. Base your response on principles of human development and diagnostic assessment.

Principles of Learning and Teaching

Write your response to Question 7 here.

_____

_____

_____

_____

_____

_____

_____

_____

_____

_____

_____

_____

_____

_____

_____

_____

_____

_____

_____

Principles of Learning and Teaching

Write your response to Question 8 here.

_____

_____

_____

_____

_____

_____

_____

_____

_____

_____

_____

_____

_____

_____

_____

_____

_____

_____

_____

Principles of Learning and Teaching

Write your response to Question 9 here.

Principles of Learning and Teaching

Write your response to Question 10 here.

_____

_____

_____

_____

_____

_____

_____

_____

_____

_____

_____

_____

_____

_____

_____

_____

_____

_____

_____

_____

_____

Principles of Learning and Teaching

Write your response to Question 11 here.

Principles of Learning and Teaching

Write your response to Question 12 here.

_____

_____

_____

_____

_____

_____

_____

_____

_____

_____

_____

_____

_____

_____

_____

_____

_____

_____

_____

_____

_____

Chapter 7

**Scoring Guides and Sample Responses
to the Practice Questions**

▶   ▶   ▶   ▶   ▶   ▶   ▶   ▶   ▶   ▶   ▶   ▶

After you have finished taking the practice test in chapter 6, review your answers in light of the question-specific scoring guides and the sample scored answers given in this chapter. If you find it difficult to evaluate your answers and assign them scores, ask a professor or practicing teacher for help.

Keep in mind while evaluating your answers that the scoring guides do not contain exhaustive lists of all possible answers. Your ideas may be acceptable if they are consistent with the question, the case, and the principles of effective teaching. The scorers are trained to count such answers as correct.

Question 1

1. **Document 1, Mr. Jenner's project plan for World Cultures Panel Presentations, demonstrates several aspects of effective instructional planning.**

   - **Identify TWO strengths of Mr. Jenner's project plan.**

   - **Explain how each strength demonstrates an aspect of effective instructional planning. Base your response on principles of effective instructional planning.**

Scoring Guide for Question 1

Score of 2

The response identifies and explains two appropriate strengths of lesson design from Document 1, such as the following:

- Mr. Jenner's direction to use characteristics of a previously studied culture helps give students a place to begin work by relating the students' new knowledge to what they already know.

- By requiring that each student participate in group planning and presentation, he ensures that each student will contribute something to the project and hear the contributions others can make, while they build the speaking and listening skills specified in the objectives.

- By requiring students to introduce relevant artifacts from art, literature, music, multimedia or other cultural objects, he helps students draw appropriate connections among disciplines and addresses his objective of using creativity.

- Mr. Jenner's assignment requires that students "plan, gather information, and present a panel report." This activity involves them in analyzing, evaluating, synthesizing, and applying data, thereby addressing his objective for students to use higher-order thinking skills.

- By forming cooperative groups for the projects and building in some aspects of positive interdependence (such as having them all speak and listen to one another, demanding all group members participate in the planning and presentation, having them produce one project for the whole group, assigning responsibilities for each group member, etc.) and then basing part of the assessment on the group work and the panel presentation, Mr. Jenner addresses cooperative learning in a cohesive way.

- The activities and the assessment are linked. Each of the three points in the assessment is linked to one or more of the activities, and all the activities except the first one are directly linked to an assessment. The first one, nevertheless, is indirectly linked.

Score of 1

The response identifies and explains one appropriate strength of lesson design, such as those presented in score point 2, or the response identifies but does not explain two appropriate strengths of lesson design.

Score of 0

The response fails to address the question, presents inappropriate strengths, or is vague.

Response that would receive a score of 2.

Mr. Jenner's project plan demonstrates several aspects of effective planning. His goals, assignment, activities, and assessment are closely related and support each other. For example, his objective of using creativity (art, literature, music, multimedia, objects) is directly supported by requirement #5 of his assignment. His objective of demonstrating speaking and listening skills, his requirement that all students must participate in group planning and presentation, and his assigning both an individual and group grade for the group work and the presentation support each other.

Commentary on the above response

The response identifies and explains two specific strengths of instructional planning evidenced in the project plan. It begins with an overall statement and then provides two specific appropriate examples that meet the requirements of the question. The response receives full credit.

Response that would receive a score of 1.

The project plan demonstrates aspects of effective planning. A very important feature of Mr. Jenner's planning is that he is building on prior knowledge. He tells the students that they are to use the characteristics of a culture studied the previous week to organize their presentations. When teachers link what has already been studied to a new task or a new concept, students have a much better opportunity for success. Building on prior knowledge is always to be desired in planning lessons, and Mr. Jenner does this well.

Commentary on the above response

The response presents a full explanation of one aspect of effective planning. The discussion presents more information about building on prior knowledge than would be necessary to answer the question, but because there is only one aspect of effective planning presented, the response receives only partial credit.

Response that would receive a score of 0.

One aspect of effective planning that I have learned is always to make your unit plan or your lesson plan well organized and easy for you to follow and for others to understand. Many people may see your lesson plan—a mentor teacher, a supervisor, your principal—and the first impression they form of your teaching may come from the lesson plan. Mr. Jenner's project plan is very well organized, presented in clear outline form, and is easy to understand and follow.

Commentary on the above response

The response does not present appropriate aspects of effective planning. The response does not provide evidence of an understanding of the concept of "effective planning" and presents a discussion only of surface features of the lesson or project plan itself. The response receives no credit.

Question 2

2. **Review the assessment section of Document 1, Mr. Jenner's project plan.**

   ■ **Suggest TWO ways in which Mr. Jenner could strengthen the assessment section of his project plan in order to provide students with a better opportunity to demonstrate their accomplishments on this project.**

   ■ **For each suggestion you made, describe how it would provide students a better opportunity to demonstrate their accomplishments on this project. Base your response on principles of formal and informal assessment.**

Scoring Guide for Question 2

Score of 2

The response presents two appropriate ways Mr. Jenner could strengthen the assessment section of his project plan to help students have a better opportunity to demonstrate their accomplishments in this project, such as the following:

   ■ He could provide rubrics for the assessment of each part, or could clearly indicate the criteria on which each part will be evaluated. This might encourage the students to include information that they might otherwise have left out.

   ■ He could indicate the relative weight of each part of the assessment. This might encourage the students to include information that they might otherwise have left out.

   ■ He could add some assessment points during the project, such as a brief assessment after the video to see if they could identify what made a presentation effective.

   ■ He could add a written assessment at the end so that individual students would have an opportunity to demonstrate what they have learned about the cultures presented and/or about the specific culture they studied.

   ■ He could add an oral assessment at the end, having students plan and present individual oral presentations on one particular aspect of the unit.

Score of 1

The response presents one appropriate way Mr. Jenner could strengthen the assessment section of his project plan and describes how it could give students a better opportunity to demonstrate their accomplishments in this project, such as those presented in score point 2, or the response suggests two appropriate ways Mr. Jenner could strengthen the assessment section without sufficient description of how that could give students a better opportunity to demonstrate their accomplishments.

Score of 0

The response fails to address the question, presents inappropriate ways to strengthen the assessment section, or is vague.

Response that would receive a score of 2.

- Add an indication of the criteria on which each assessment will be made—students need to know more than the names or kinds of the assessments—they need to know on what their work will be evaluated. Their final products could be more complete as a result.

- Add an assessment at the end, so each student has another opportunity to demonstrate what has been learned, either about all the cultures reported on or about the specific culture the student studied.

Commentary on the above response

The response presents, in sufficient detail, two appropriate ways he could strengthen the assessment section. Bulleted responses presenting appropriate information can receive full credit.

Response that would receive a score of 1.

He could add another assessment toward the beginning to be sure students begin to understand what an effective panel is. Before showing the video of the panel, he could tell students that as soon as it is over, they are to explain what they saw that they thought was effective. This would assess both their viewing and listening skills, and their ability to figure out what effective panels are.

Commentary on the above response

The response presents only one appropriate way he could strengthen the assessment section. It therefore receives partial credit.

Response that would receive a score of 0.

He could add a reading assignment. It looks to me like students are going to just do the group work and share all their ideas. But they would do a much better job if he assigned some reading, so that they would have more information to draw on. This would help strengthen the knowledge about cultures that they have.

Commentary on the above response

The response does not address the question. Suggesting an additional activity, even though that activity might have been assessed in some way, does not meet the requirement posed by the question. It receives no credit.

Question 3

3. **Assume that Mr. Jenner and Mr. Rose discuss the beginning of the class that Mr. Rose observed, with the focus on the first few minutes when students enter the room, before they begin to move to cooperative groups.**

   ■ **Suggest TWO strategies Mr. Rose might recommend that Mr. Jenner use to make the transition from lunch to class smoother and less disruptive.**

   ■ **Explain how each strategy you suggested could improve the transition from lunch to class, making it smoother and less disruptive. Base your response on principles of classroom management.**

Scoring Guide for Question 3

Score of 2

The response suggests and explains two appropriate strategies for Mr. Jenner to make the transition from lunch to class smoother and less disruptive, such as the following:

■ Mr. Jenner can establish a routine for the opening of each class. He could pose a short problem or issue, presenting it on the board or on an overhead projector. Each student would have to deal with it in the first three minutes of class in order to get credit. This exercise can reinforce the idea that students must come to class on time and begin work right away.

■ Mr. Jenner could have established clear-cut rules for behavior in his class early in the year, discussed them with the class, and posted them in the room indicating what the consequences are of breaking them. This should have created an orderly beginning class routine by late September.

■ Mr. Jenner could stop the class, have a discussion with them about the problems the disruptive behavior causes, and establish orderly procedures for beginning class with the input of the students.

■ Mr. Jenner could stand by the door, greet students individually by name, and then direct them to be seated. In this way, he could break up potentially disruptive pairs or groups, and establish a clear sense of order from the time they enter the room.

- On the previous day, Mr. Jenner could have discussed with the students the importance of getting to work immediately when class starts because the task will demand all of the period to complete. This sets an expectation of work from the first to the last moment of class.

- Rather than addressing problems in a loud and public way, Mr. Jenner could move quickly to the location of problems, speak directly and clearly to the students, and insist that they take their seats.

- Mr. Jenner can establish a rule that each student be in his/her seat and ready to work when the bell rings. To support this rule, he needs to convey a clear set of consequences that are quietly, firmly, and consistently applied. This makes the misbehavior, rather than Mr. Jenner's impatience, the rationale for the consequence or punishment.

Score of 1

The response suggests and explains one strategy for Mr. Jenner to make the transition from lunch to class smoother and less disruptive, such as those presented in score point 2, or the response suggests but does not sufficiently explain two appropriate strategies to make the transition from lunch to class smoother and less disruptive.

Score of 0

The response fails to address the question, presents inappropriate strategies, or is vague.

Response that would receive a score of 2.

Mr. Jenner needs to establish rules and routines for his class. One way he can accomplish this is to discuss with his students early in the year the rules of behavior and the consequences of misbehavior. Those rules and routines should be posted in the classroom and Mr. Jenner needs to be consistent and fair in enforcing the rules and routines until they become automatic for his students. At this point in the year, he can change his behavior by standing by the door to greet each student individually, to direct them politely but firmly to be seated and get ready to work, and to address potential problems as they arise. In addition, he can have an assignment posted on the board that they are to complete within the first few minutes of class.

Commentary on the above response

The response presents two appropriate strategies to make the transition smoother and less disruptive. They are presented in clear detail and are directly applicable to the situation presented in the case. The response receives full credit.

Response that would receive a score of 1.

Mr. Jenner needs to have something specific for the students to do as soon as the bell rings. In some cases this is called "a starter." If he has a short 3–5 minute assignment posted on the board when the students come in, if he collects the work as soon as the time is up, if the work is something that will engage the students, and if there is a clear assessment or "reward" system in place, students are far more likely to come in and get to work. Because they are not directly responsible for doing anything for the first few minutes, they believe they are free to wander around the room and have social time.

Commentary on the above response

The response presents one appropriate strategy to make the transition smoother, but does not present two strategies as required by the question. The response receives partial credit.

Response that would receive a score of 0.

This is only the fourth week of school. Students are still getting used to being back from vacation and getting reacquainted with each other. They are also getting to know their teachers. If Mr. Jenner is patient, within a few more weeks students will realize that there is lots to learn and they need to control themselves. Cracking down now will only antagonize the students and he may lose his chances for helping them learn.

Commentary on the above response

The response presents an inappropriate course of action, which is essentially to ignore the problem. The question directs that responses should be based on principles of effective classroom management and effective instructional planning. The response does not do this and receives no credit.

Question 4

4. **Document 2, the transcript of the class and Mr. Rose's notations, indicates that Mr. Jenner could improve his use of cooperative groups.**

   - **Suggest TWO strategies that Mr. Rose might recommend that Mr. Jenner implement to make the cooperative groups work more effectively.**

   - **Explain how the use of each strategy you suggested could make the cooperative groups work more effectively. Base your response on principles of planning instruction and classroom management.**

Scoring Guide for Question 4

Score of 2

The response suggests and explains two specific appropriate strategies Mr. Jenner can use to make his cooperative groups work more effectively, such as the following:

- Mr. Jenner can have a list of who is in each group on the board when the students enter so all students know which group they're in immediately.

- Mr. Jenner can make it clear when groups are assigned that no one can change groups. This policy can be reinforced by a statement accompanying the list of groups on the board.

- In addition to giving the students the assignment sheet the day before, Mr. Jenner can give each group one copy of the assignment, which one of them must read aloud as soon as they meet so that everyone knows what the group is to do.

- Mr. Jenner can require that each group produce a quick product that specifically requires each group member's participation within the first 2–3 minutes of class. This requires the groups to go to work immediately, to reinforce their own discipline, and to make sure all group members are working with them.

- When he assigns the groups and when he reviews group membership on the board, Mr. Jenner can assign individual roles to each group member along with what each role requires in terms of group behavior/performance.

- Mr. Jenner can spend the first few minutes of class reviewing the roles and responsibilities of each person in a group to make sure that there will be little confusion later when the groups are working.

- Mr. Jenner can provide a rubric or specific assessment plan that indicates how individual and group grades will be assigned, reinforcing the roles that have been assigned and the notion of all members working cooperatively together.

Score of 1

The response suggests and explains one appropriate strategy Mr. Jenner can use to make his cooperative groups work more effectively, such as those presented in score point 2, or the response suggests but does not sufficiently explain two appropriate strategies Mr. Jenner can use to make the cooperative groups work more effectively.

Score of 0

The response fails to address the question, presents inappropriate strategies, or is vague.

Response that would receive a score of 2.

Mr. Jenner understands some of the basic principles of forming cooperative groups, but he needs to build in more specific individual responsibility to make the groups operate more effectively. He can assign specific roles with specific responsibilities, and can tie these directly and publicly to his assessment criteria. He could also post on the board a list of who is in each group and what responsibility each person has, to make transition to the beginning of group work smoother. In addition, he might review the roles and responsibilities in the first few minutes in order to make sure all students know what they are to do in their groups.

Commentary on the above response

The response suggests and explains appropriate strategies Mr. Jenner might use to make the use of cooperative groups more effective. The strategies are clear and specific. The question calls for two strategies; providing a third strategy does not earn extra credit. The response receives full credit.

Response that would receive a score of 1.

The first thing Mr. Jenner could have done was to give the students a handout with the roles and responsibilities of each person in the group. That way each person will know what is expected and will be more ready to go to work. The second thing he could have done was to post the same information on a big display on the bulletin board. This would let the students know that the information is really important.

Commentary on the above response

The response presents the same strategy twice. Repeating the same strategy with a slight variation does not constitute a full response to the requirement to explain "<u>two</u> strategies...." The response receives partial credit.

Response that would receive a score of 0.

Two strategies Mr. Jenner could use are first to be a little calmer with his students. Group work is supposed to be "cooperative," and he is setting up a hostile environment. The second strategy is to mix the groups up a little bit. By always having the same students work together, he does not give the students opportunities to work collaboratively with a variety of people.

Commentary on the above response

The first "strategy" presented is not responsive to the question, which calls for strategies to make cooperative group work more effective. The second point, while it may be valid in a different question about the long-term use of cooperative groups, is not related to the facts of the case and is not responsive to the question. The response receives no credit.

Question 5

5. **Review Document 3, Mr. Jenner's conversation with Ms. Young, in which he says the students in the class are "not typical" of students their age and she implies that perhaps they are.**

   ■ **Identify TWO individual or group behaviors described in Document 2 (the transcript of the class) and/or Document 5 (the student responses) that are typical of students ages 12 to 13.**

   ■ **For each behavior you identified, describe how it is typical of students ages 12 to 13. Base your response on principles of human development.**

Scoring Guide for Question 5

Score of 2

The response presents two appropriate behaviors exhibited by individuals or groups and for each behavior explains how it is typical of students ages 12 to 13, such as the following:

■ The loud conversation and socializing are very typical behavior for 12 and 13 year olds whenever there is a lull in whatever else they are supposed to be doing. They are very interested in one another since friends are important to them.

■ Kim's melodramatic suggestion that she has a concussion is an exaggeration for effect that is typical of many 12 and 13 year olds' behavior.

■ The boys' rambunctiousness and inability to sit still are typical of the age group. Even when sitting "still," early adolescents sometimes have a hard time not tapping a foot or a finger or squirming in a seat.

■ Javier's stealing Christi's backpack in order to get a response and Christi's attempt to get Mr. Jenner to intervene on her behalf is a typical 12 and 13 year old interchange. A student of one sex tries to annoy a student of the opposite sex to get a response and the second student feigns helplessness and asks an authority figure to "rescue" him or her.

■ Tony's desire to have Mr. Jenner act as an enforcer of rules is typical of an early teen's sense that there is right and wrong and if the adults will just make that clear to everyone, everything will work out well.

■ Leroy's sense of martyrdom from Mr. Jenner's attempts to enforce the rules is also typical 12 and 13 year old behavior. Students this age often say that what adults call misbehavior is just a misunderstanding of teenagers.

Score of 1

The response presents one appropriate behavior exhibited by individuals or groups and for the behavior explains why it is typical of students ages 12 to 13, such as those presented in score point 2, or the response identifies two behaviors exhibited by individuals or groups but does not explain how each is typical of students ages 12 to 13.

Score of 0

The response fails to address the question, presents inappropriate examples of behavior or inappropriate explanations, or is vague.

Response that would receive a score of 2.

Mr. Jenner's students are rambunctious, social creatures, exhibiting behavior that is typical of twelve- and thirteen-year-olds. Even when supposedly "still," many twelve- and thirteen-year-olds cannot keep from tapping a foot, a finger, or a pencil or squirming and/or twitching in their seats. Mr. Jenner's highly active students are quite typical of students this age who are constantly in action. Another trait of the age group is to talk with one another because they are most interested in what their friends are thinking or doing and want to react to them. The need for social acceptance is great, and Mr. Jenner's students' behavior illustrates this need.

Commentary on the above response

The response presents two behaviors exhibited by individuals or groups in the case and for each explains why it is typical of students this age. The behaviors are appropriately selected and clearly tied to adolescent growth and development. The response receives full credit.

Response that would receive a score of 1.

Kim is really typical of students this age. She is very theatrical and makes a big deal out of what has happened. Students this age often love to exaggerate problems, either because they think it is funny or because they want attention. Kim's behavior is typical. Actually, when you look at it, all the kids in the class are typical of students this age. Mr. Jenner is really wrong when he says he doesn't think these kids are typical. Everything they do is behavior I have seen middle school kids exhibiting.

Commentary on the above response

The first point, while brief, does identify a behavior of one of the students and makes a case for the behavior being typical of students this age. However, the second point is a broad generalization and is not responsive to the question. The response receives partial credit.

Response that would receive a score of 0.

I don't think there is any such thing as behavior that is "typical" of students of any age. Every student is an individual. Every student has different motivations, different background, different hopes and dreams. I believe in treating each student as a unique being. By lumping them all together, you miss the qualities and characteristics that make each of them unique.

Commentary on the above response

The response does not reveal the kind of knowledge of human growth and development called for by the INTASC standards. While it is true that the standards acknowledge "individual variations" within patterns of developmental progression, an appropriate response to the question is not to refute accepted principles of human growth and development. The response receives no credit.

Question 6

6. **Assume that Mr. Jenner has read all of the student responses to the assignment on improving classroom behavior (Document 4).**

   - **Suggest TWO additional actions Mr. Jenner might take to further involve the class in improving classroom behavior.**

   - **For each action you suggested, explain how it is likely to be effective in improving classroom behavior. Base your response on principles of communication and classroom management.**

Scoring Guide for Question 6

Score of 2

The response suggests and explains two appropriate actions Mr. Jenner might take to further involve the class in improving classroom behavior, such as the following:

   - Mr. Jenner might read aloud some of the comments, both positive and negative, that students wrote without identifying authors. He could then carry out a class discussion about some solutions to the issues raised by the student comments, asking them to begin by identifying two or three that seem most reasonable and useful, thereby involving the class in the solution to the problem.

   - Mr. Jenner might have his cooperative groups discuss the problem as identified in the student comments, which he presents on a hand-out with students' names removed. He could ask each group to review proposed solutions and then have the groups prioritize the options. They could then report to the full class, and the class could recommend which options would become the class rules and procedures.

- Mr. Jenner could list each of the problems and each of the solutions proposed by the students on the board or on an overhead. He could then have a class discussion about which behaviors are the most problematic and which solutions make the most sense. He could then give each student a pad of Post-it notes and ask each student to indicate which problems are the most troublesome personally and which solutions are best from his or her perspective. In this way, Mr. Jenner could begin to build consensus about problems and solutions.

- Since Mr. Jenner's subject is social studies, he could devise a typical democratic solution. He could appoint a judicial board of students. That board could be charged with reading all the student responses and solutions and proposing some procedures, routines, and rules for the class as well as punishments for breaking them. This would offer a practical lesson in judicial review and bring an element of peer review into the process.

- Mr. Jenner could make a list of the things that prevent members of the class from paying attention and some solutions based on what the students wrote. He could then take a vote on what the most problematic behaviors are and what the best solutions are to those problems. The solutions could then be enacted as the rules and responsibilities in his class.

- He could draw on his subject matter, social studies, and have students develop a constitution with rights and responsibilities for members of the group.

Score of 1

The response suggests and explains one appropriate action Mr. Jenner might take to further involve the class in improving classroom behavior such as those presented in score point 2, or the response suggests but does not sufficiently explain two appropriate actions Mr. Jenner might take to further involve the class in improving classroom behavior.

Score of 0

The response fails to address the question, presents inappropriate steps, or is vague.

Response that would receive a score of 2.

By asking his students what they think the problems are and what might be done to solve them, he has the necessary data to reach a resolution by involving his students. He might list the problems and the solutions on the board and either discuss viable solutions with his class or have the class discuss them in cooperative groups. In either case, they ought to be able to reach some consensus about the most problematic behaviors and the most reasonable solutions. He might also have them talk about what a constitution is, and then have them draw up a constitution listing their rights and responsibilities, since this is a social studies class.

Commentary on the above response

The response presents two thoughtful, appropriate actions Mr. Jenner might take. The steps are appropriate in terms of the case and the assignment Mr. Jenner has given, and are explained in detail. The response receives full credit.

Response that would receive a score of 1.

Since this is a social studies class, Mr. Jenner might turn to principles of democracy to help him figure out what to do next. He could reinforce the notion of groups of people making their own rules and the notion of a "society" being one in which people agree to abide by those rules. He could therefore give the students the "raw material" of what has been written in response to the class assignment, and working together they could review them all, perhaps prioritize them, and then come to consensus about which of them might be most useful in solving the problem. In this way, he has modeled democracy in action and has begun to solve the problem.

Commentary on the above response

The response presents one appropriate action Mr. Jenner might take. However, because the question calls for two appropriate actions, the response receives only partial credit.

Response that would receive a score of 0.

What Mr. Jenner should do next is to analyze very carefully all the responses he has received. Of course, he is going to receive some like Leroy's that he might set aside as he works to create a sensible solution to the problem. He wants to honor what the serious, thoughtful students have said. Therefore, if he lists all the positive suggestions, and tabulates for himself the number of times each suggestion is made, he will begin to see a pattern. From this pattern, he can develop a set of clear rules that reflect the students' thinking.

Commentary on the above response

The question asks for actions he might take "to further involve the class in improving...." The solution presented does not meet the requirement of involving the class. Rather, it places all action and responsibility with the teacher. It is therefore not an appropriate step and receives no credit.

Question 7

7. In his self-analysis, Mr. Payton says that the better-performing students say small-group work is boring and that they learn more working alone or only with students like themselves. Assume Mr. Payton wants to continue using cooperative learning groups because he believes they have value for all students.

- Identify TWO strategies Mr. Payton could use to address the concerns of the students who complained and to make cooperative group work more effective.

- For each strategy you identified, explain how its use could address the concerns of the students who complained and could make group work more effective. Base your response on principles of effective instructional strategies.

Scoring Guide for Question 7

Score of 2

The response identifies and explains two appropriate strategies Mr. Payton can use to address the concerns of the students who have complained, such as the following:

- Mr. Payton can make each of the groups interdependent by giving each student an assigned role and checking to make sure each student fulfills that role. He can be sure that the better-performing students have roles that will challenge their skills and abilities, without always having them in a position in which they can dominate the group.

- Mr. Payton can make sure each student must produce an independent product as a result of working together. In that way, those who do their work more carefully and thoughtfully will not be penalized by those who do not take the work as seriously.

- Mr. Payton can ask the bright students, like Burns, not to speak during the group work, but to record and listen to what others have to say. He can then make sure the recorders are the ones who speak for the group, ensuring that the recorders hear what the others say and present it accurately. That will encourage the less able students to speak up and the most able students to have a crucial role.

- Mr. Payton can use a jigsaw cooperative learning group approach. First, the more able students work together in cooperative groups, assigned the most sophisticated material to consider or to learn. The less able or less motivated students have important but less complex issues to consider or tasks to complete. Then when the more able and motivated students return to the heterogeneous group, they must share their ideas in a way others will understand, and they learn from the other students ideas and insights they have been exploring.

- Mr. Payton can give each group only one copy of the problem the group is to work on, and explain that the group should work together so that everyone in the group understands the material equally well. He could indicate that reporting will be done by calling on a reporter randomly, and indicate that a group grade will be given based on the reporter's information. This interdependence demands that each member have an equally strong interest in each member of the group understanding the material.

- Mr. Payton can require that each member of the class spend ten minutes writing down what she or he thinks before the groups are formed. He can assign credit first for these ideas submitted to him. He can then ask the groups to spend the first ten minutes of their work listening to what others have already written and selecting some of the best ideas to work on in the group exercise. This technique provides credit for the individual work of the more able and motivated students, and provides them an opportunity to share their ideas with other members of the group and have those ideas valued.

Score of 1

The response identifies and explains one appropriate strategy that Mr. Payton can use to address the concerns of the students who have complained, such as those presented in score point 2, or the response identifies but does not sufficiently explain two appropriate strategies that Mr. Payton can use to address the concerns of the students who have complained.

Score of 0

The response fails to address the question, presents inappropriate strategies, or is vague.

Response that would receive a score of 2.

Mr. Payton has to be creative to find strategies that will address the concerns of the students who have complained and still support the strengths of cooperative learning. One way he can do that is to assign these students a variety of roles in which they can share their insights and knowledge with others in a way that will provide them recognition and will help other students. He can also build specific requirements that provide for individual work into the cooperative work, either before the groups meet or as the groups are working. This individual work provides the more able or motivated students with an opportunity to demonstrate their insights and knowledge and be given appropriate credit for them. The individual work can also serve as a basis for the group work.

Commentary on the above response

The response presents two appropriate strategies that Mr. Payton can use to address the concerns of the students who have complained. Acknowledging that this is not an easy task and that he has to be "creative," the response then presents two specific approaches or strategies in detail. The response receives full credit.

Response that would receive a score of 1.

I understand why these students are concerned. But Mr. Payton shouldn't just give up on cooperative learning groups. I had a situation like this, when four really bright and eager kids just didn't want to work with students who were less able or less motivated. One thing he could do would be to assign his groups very carefully, so that one of the complaining kids is in each group. He could then use a system where he begins the cooperative work by regrouping, numbering the kids in each group 1, 2, 3, 4. First, all the "1's" work together, all the "2's" work together, and so forth. All the kids who complained would have the same number. After they have had the opportunity to work together on an advanced level, the groups would reform. The "1's" could go back to their own groups and share with them what the "1" group came up with. In this way, they have the intellectual stimulation of working together first, and then the status of sharing with other kids.

Commentary on the above response

The response presents a detailed explanation of one strategy to address the concerns. While it is presented in considerable detail, it is still only one strategy. Since the question calls for two strategies, the response receives partial credit.

Question 8

8. Review the section "Background information on lesson to be observed by supervisor" in which Mr. Payton describes the modifications he made to the lesson for Jimmy and Burns.

    ■   **Suggest TWO other modifications, one for Jimmy and one for Burns, that Mr. Payton could have made that would have offered the students a better learning situation.**

    ■   **For each modification you suggested, explain how the modification could have provided Jimmy or Burns a better learning situation. Base your response on principles of varied instruction for diverse learners.**

Scoring Guide for Question 8

Score of 2

The response suggests and explains an appropriate modification for each of two of the students, such as the following:

   ■   Mr. Payton might talk with Jimmy about the ways he has received information and the ways he has been expected to show what he has learned in the past. He can then try to provide him with alternate assignments and assessments. For example, if reading is a problem, he might find information that is recorded or on video for Jimmy. If writing is a problem, he might offer Jimmy ways to demonstrate understanding orally.

- Jimmy has specifically indicated he has problems "remembering a lot of dates and stuff," so Mr. Payton might stress other aspects of history where Jimmy might concentrate. He might specifically identify concepts and kinds of events that could engage Jimmy, providing information and assessing Jimmy's understanding about them.

- Mr. Payton might offer Jimmy some graphic organizers in order to understand the facts and important ideas about Catherine the Great. Jimmy may have problems organizing and remembering information and needs help in this area.

- Mr. Payton might offer Burns a much more sophisticated book or other material on Catherine the Great. He could ask him to read it and prepare a class in which he teaches what he discovers to other students either in a small group or in class. This might engage Burns at a more sophisticated level.

- Mr. Payton might ask Burns to develop a means to communicate what he knows to those students who are struggling, perhaps using technology to create an interesting and informative presentation. That would challenge Burns to rethink the material in a more complex way and to find ways to communicate more effectively.

- Mr. Payton might ask Burns to report on his travel and interest in international affairs, linking those interests to his understanding of Catherine the Great. This would relate the study of history to his interests and provide a means for him to share his interests and knowledge with others.

Score of 1

The response suggests and explains an appropriate modification for one student, such as those presented in score point 2, or the response suggests but does not sufficiently explain appropriate modifications for each of the two students.

Score of 0

The response fails to address the question, presents inappropriate modifications, or is vague.

Response that would receive a score of 2.

For Burns, who is a bright, independent learner, providing him the opportunity to take extra responsibility for mastering challenging material and figuring out how to help his classmates understand it might help him to be more open and positive in his classroom behavior. For example, he might use more complex materials to access information, or might create a program using technology to share his knowledge and insights with others. For Jimmy, Mr. Payton might have a conference with him to find out how he was expected to learn social studies in the past and why he is so accepting of failing social studies. This conference may lead to a strategy such as the use of information presented visually or orally, or the use of graphic organizers to access information, or an alternate means of demonstrating his understanding if written assessments are part of the problem.

Commentary on the above response

The response explains for each identified student one appropriate way Mr. Payton might have provided modification. The strategies are specific and appropriate for the student under consideration. The response receives full credit.

Response that would receive a score of 1.

Jimmy is a very interesting student to consider. He has a history of failure and seems to accept the fact that he may fail again. However, he seems quite outgoing so he might be willing to try if approached right. I think the first thing Mr. Payton could do would be to sit down and talk with him. He needs to try to figure out why Jimmy failed in the past. He might ask him if he has any ideas about how he learns best—and things teachers have had him do that don't help him. Then, with this information, Mr. Payton might be able to come up with some approaches based on Jimmy's learning style. If Jimmy says he hates to read, Mr. Payton needs to find a way for him to access the information other than reading! Another thing Mr. Payton might do is adjust what he expects Jimmy to learn. Jimmy says he has problems with "a lot of dates and stuff." But he may be interested in other aspects of history—why people did the things they did, for example. By tailoring the study of history to aspects that might be more appropriate for Jimmy, Mr. Payton might have a better chance of helping Jimmy succeed.

Commentary on the above response

The response presents two strategies for one student identified in the question, rather than one strategy for each of the two identified students. Responses must address the specific questions posed. Since the question specifies the response is to provide modifications for the two different identified students, and this response presents modifications for only one student, it receives partial credit.

Response that follows would receive a score of 0.

I think the modification he should make for both students is to be much clearer about what the expectations of the course are. Sometimes students are tuned out or bored because they just don't know what is expected of them. Maybe Mr. Payton needs to post his expectations prominently in the room so that both of these students can see what is expected. The expectations also need to indicate what is required for passing, so that Jimmy and Burns will know what the limits are.

Commentary on the above response

The response does not present appropriate modifications for the students. Because the response does not address the question as it is posed, it receives no credit.

Question 9

9. Mr. Payton's second and third goals are "To link students' textbook reading to other sources of information" and "To give students practice in combining information from written and oral material."

    ▪ Suggest TWO strategies and/or activities Mr. Payton could use to help his students work toward meeting one or both of these goals.

    ▪ For each strategy or activity you suggested, explain how its use could help students work toward meeting Mr. Payton's second and/or third goal(s). Base your response on principles of effective instructional planning and strategies.

Scoring Guide for Question 9

Score of 2

The response suggests and explains two appropriate strategies Mr. Payton could use to help students work toward meeting one or both of these goals, such as the following:

▪ Have students gain information individually or in pairs on Catherine from a variety of print and non-print sources, and have each individual or group report briefly on what was learned. Hold the students responsible for the materials presented in an assessment.

▪ Form cooperative groups and give each group a different brief text about Catherine. Have each group share ideas contained in the text and then organize the information gained into a presentation to the class. Mr. Payton can build the information from the groups into his assessment.

▪ Gather several portraits of Catherine. Have pairs of students discuss with one another what features of Catherine each painter has captured and what made them think that way. Then, conduct a whole class discussion about the different portraits and what they say about Catherine. In the final assessment, make sure the students link what they learned from the discussion of the portraits with what they learned from the textbook.

▪ Select several short, contemporary accounts of Catherine that represent different perspectives. Let the students study the accounts overnight. Then, conduct a discussion about how different people see the Russian ruler and why. Have the students draw comparisons and contrasts to the perspectives offered in the textbook and contemporary accounts.

▪ Bring in a film strip or a movie about Catherine. After showing it to the class, form groups to discuss what the students saw—what supported and was different from what the lectures and the textbook presented. Mr. Payton could then ask each student to write a paper about Catherine emphasizing the aspects that seem most significant after studying different sources.

Score of 1

The response offers one appropriate strategy for Mr. Payton to work toward one or both of these goals, such as those presented in score point 2, or the response suggests but does not sufficiently explain two appropriate strategies Mr. Payton could use to work toward one or both of these goals.

Score of 0

The response fails to address the question, presents inappropriate strategies, or is vague.

Response that would receive a score of 2.

Mr. Payton can

- bring in other sources—contemporary accounts of Catherine or a variety of commentaries about her reign—and have the students discuss those sources in comparison to the text and the lectures. Encourage students to notice the different points of view that emerge about Catherine.

- use audio-visual materials or technology to enable students to access additional information about Catherine. Compare what has been learned in this way to the material from the text and lectures.

Commentary on the above response

Responses may be in a variety of formats. They do not need to be in paragraph form or in complete sentences. The response presents two appropriate strategies Mr. Payton could use to link students' textbook reading to other sources. They are specific and address his goal directly. The response receives full credit.

Response that would receive a score of 1.

One thing he could do would be to find a lot of pictures of Catherine. The students have already formed an impression through reading of what she was like. He could use small groups, give each group a picture, and ask them to discuss the impression they get of her from the picture, and then compare and contrast that impression to ideas they have received from their textbook.

A second thing he could do would be to take the textbook account, and then pretend they were writing a different textbook giving a different impression of Catherine. They could write the same account from a different slant, to see that textbooks are not "the truth," but rather the author's version of "the truth."

Commentary on the above response

The response presents one appropriate strategy that addresses the question and one that does not address the question. The goal being addressed is "to link students' textbook reading to other sources of information." The first strategy presents an appropriate way to do this, but the second strategy relies only on the textbook. Although it might be an appropriate strategy for another purpose, it is not responsive to the question. The response therefore receives partial credit.

Response that would receive a score of 0.

There are many ways teachers can link students' textbook reading to other sources of information. There are so many sources of information available to teachers and students, especially in the history/social studies area. With the help of a librarian or media center specialist, a teacher can locate lots and lots of really interesting and informative material. More and more, students are not relying solely on the textbook, and that's a very good thing. We are in the technology age, and we should teach that way.

Commentary on the above response

The response fails to address the question which calls for two strategies or activities to meet his goal. The answer is general and vague and receives no credit.

Question 10

10. **Mr. Payton's fourth goal is "To give students experience in note-taking." Review the description of Wednesday's lesson and Mr. Payton's reflection on the lesson.**

- **Suggest TWO additional strategies Mr. Payton could have used during the lecture to help all students take notes in a way that would support them as learners.**

- **For each strategy you suggested, explain how its use could help all students take notes in a way that would support them as learners. Base your response on principles of effective instruction.**

Scoring Guide for Question 10

Score of 2

The response suggests and explains two additional appropriate strategies Mr. Payton can use during the lecture to help all students take notes in a way that will support them as learners, such as the following:

- Mr. Payton can use an overhead projector with a paper covering the outline of the topics he has yet to cover. As he takes up each topic, he can move the cover paper down so the students can see the next step in the outline he has prepared and can address that topic in their notes.

- Mr. Payton can offer the students a skeletal outline with enough space in which to write additional notes. This can serve as a guide to help students know what is important to take down in the notes.

- Mr. Payton can outline the lecture on the board so students can see what he thinks is important and ask the students to copy the outline as well as take notes on the additional material they think is important.

- Mr. Payton can stop the lecture whenever he is changing topics and ask one or two students to summarize the important points he's already made. This gives each student a second chance to hear the important points and to get them down in the notes.

- Mr. Payton can give the students a skeletal outline of the important material. Before he covers a topic he can ask students to summarize the important points made in the text and in any other sources. He can then ask the students to take notes on the material in the lecture that takes a different point of view toward Catherine.

- Mr. Payton could stop frequently during his lecture, and in a space provided on a separate study guide could identify where they are in the lecture and ask each student to write one quiz or test question that would address the points made in the lecture.

Score of 1

The response suggests and explains one additional appropriate strategy Mr. Payton can use during the lecture to help all students take notes in a way that will support them as learners, such as those presented in score point 2, or the response suggests but does not sufficiently explain two additional appropriate strategies Mr. Payton can use during the lecture to help students take notes in a way that will support them as learners.

Score of 0

The response fails to address the question, presents inappropriate strategies, or is vague.

Response that would receive a score of 2.

There are many ways for Mr. Payton to help his students take better notes to help them as learners. One is to provide them with a skeletal outline of what he will say. Before he discusses a topic, he should have class volunteers provide information on these topics supplied by the text. He can then have students take further notes on the different aspects of Catherine that his lecture emphasizes. This will help his students focus on important contrasts between different historians. He can also have his students orally summarize the points they have written in their notes, or pose a question that would address an important idea from the notes.

Commentary on the above response

The response presents two appropriate additional strategies he could have used during the lecture. Both strategies would help students organize, understand, and remember the points covered. The response receives full credit.

Response that would receive a score of 1.

The first thing Mr. Payton could do is to stop the lecture frequently, especially when he is moving from one point to the next, and ask students to summarize what has been said. As he and other students clarify and refine the points being covered, students can add to or modify their notes. By having fuller, more accurate notes, and by having heard the material covered again in a discussion format, the students may have a better chance to understand and remember it. The second thing he could do is to be sure all students can hear, understand, and follow him. Often teachers talk too quickly and pay no attention to whether the students are with them. He needs to speak slowly and distinctly, and to do some checking to be sure students are taking notes and that the notes are accurate and complete.

Commentary on the above response

The response presents one additional appropriate strategy he could use to help all students take notes in a way that will help them as learners. However, the second point is merely a repeat of what was already presented in the case, and does not therefore constitute an "additional" strategy. The response receives partial credit.

Response that would receive a score of 0.

Here are some things Mr. Payton could do to help students during lectures so they can take better notes:

1. First, he needs to make sure there are desks for students who are left-handed. I am left-handed, and when I have to sit at a right-handed desk I just can't write very well and my notes are messy.

2. He should grade the notes. I believe that everything worth doing in class is worth assessing. Why should students sit there taking notes if they don't get any credit for them? If notes are graded, they will be better.

3. He should let students sit where they want to. If I have to sit next to someone who is very distracting, I can't take good notes. If I sit by people I know and like, I do better.

Commentary on the above response

The response presents ideas that are not responsive to the question that calls for "additional strategies he could use during the lecture to help all students take notes." Responses that use the question as an opportunity to advocate private agendas, rather than addressing the question posed, receive no credit.

Question 11

11. **Mr. Payton comments in his reflection that he is not satisfied with just a test as a "fair measure of all they do."**

- **Suggest TWO additional informal or formal assessment techniques Mr. Payton could use to provide his students with opportunities to demonstrate their learning.**

- **For each technique you suggested, describe the kind(s) of information about student learning it could provide. Base your response on principles of informal and formal assessment.**

Scoring Guide for Question 11

Score of 2

The response suggests two additional appropriate formal and/or informal assessments Mr. Payton can use and describes the kinds of information that could be provided by the assessments, such as the following:

- If he has students work in cooperative groups to interpret the different sources used to present Catherine the Great, he can have each student write an individual essay making use of different sources to support the position the student takes about the Russian ruler.

- If he assigns different sources to different groups, he can assess how well each group works with their sources by developing a rubric addressing the accuracy, completeness, and appropriateness of the information they have identified.

- After all the material has been presented about Catherine, he can have each student write a story about Catherine the Great using the points of view and facts of several of the commentators or analysts.

- He can assign a creative project in which each student is to assume the role of someone in Catherine's court and write about her from that perspective, including references to actual events and other people from the court.

- If he presents different paintings of Catherine and has pairs of students discuss them and present their ideas, he can create a study guide in which each student records the ideas presented, and he can then evaluate the study guides on a rubric provided.

- He can offer a new document about Catherine that the students have never seen before. He can then ask each student to compare and contrast, either formally or informally, the other interpretations of Catherine with the one found in this document.

■ He can list a few short quotations about Catherine on the board and ask each student to agree or disagree with one of the statements, writing about their reasons for their position and using several of the sources studied to support that position.

Score of 1

The response suggests one additional appropriate formal and/or informal assessment Mr. Payton can use and describes the kinds of information that could be provided by the assessment, such as those presented in score point 2, or the response suggests two additional appropriate assessments Mr. Payton can use but does not describe the kinds of information that could be provided by the assessment.

Score of 0

The response fails to address the question, presents inappropriate additional assessments, or is vague.

Response that would receive a score of 2.

Mr. Payton can use several different types of formal and informal assessment to check how well his students have understood what they have done during the week to study Catherine the Great. If he forms cooperative groups and asks them to analyze different sources and report their findings to the class, he can devise a rubric to assess how well each group understands and presents their interpretation of Catherine the Great. By offering a new document about Catherine that the students have not seen before, and asking them to interpret it either collectively or individually, he can determine how well students are able to work with and think critically about different sources.

Commentary on the above response

The response presents two additional types of assessment and, for each, describes the kinds of information that can be obtained from the assessment. Each is appropriate and related to the case as it is presented. The response receives full credit.

Response that would receive a score of 1.

The first thing Mr. Payton could do would be to gather a lot of quotations about Catherine the Great from a variety of sources. The quotations could address different aspects of Catherine and her reign. He could post these on the board, show them with an overhead projector, or put them on a handout for the students. The second thing he could do would be to ask the students to select one or two of these quotations and respond to them, saying why they agree or disagree with the quotation and why. Doing this would reveal their knowledge about Catherine and her reign, and also help the students improve their critical thinking skills.

Commentary on the above response

The response presents one strategy, although the wording suggests it is two. The two parts are sequential and so closely related they cannot be credited as two different strategies. The response, therefore, receives partial credit.

Response that would receive a score of 0.

I would have to have more information about Mr. Payton, the school, and the students in order to answer the question. It is not appropriate to create "cookie-cutter" lessons that can fit anyone. Without a great deal more information, it is not possible to suggest appropriate additional types of assessment.

Commentary on the above response

The response fails to address the question. Responses that say more information is needed in order to answer the question receive no credit.

Question 12

12. **Assume that Mr. Payton tells Pauline's counselor that he feels they need to learn more about Pauline as a learner so he can help her more effectively.**

   - **Describe TWO aspects of Pauline's behavior that Mr. Payton and Pauline's counselor might discuss in order to understand Pauline better as a learner.**

   - **For each aspect you described, suggest one hypothesis they might investigate to understand Pauline better as a learner. Base your response on principles of human development and diagnostic assessment.**

Scoring Guide for Question 12

Score of 2

The response presents two aspects of her behavior they might review, and for each aspect suggests one hypothesis about her as a learner, such as the following:

   - She displays no behavior problems when left alone, but appears not to be popular with the other students. One hypothesis to explore is that she has an emotional or behavioral disorder that causes her to withdraw and behave negatively to other students.

   - She stares out the window when she should be working. One hypothesis is that she has a learning disability or a behavior disorder that prevents her from focusing on work for any period of time. This could cause her to remove herself from what she sees as an unpleasant environment.

- She is hostile when spoken to about her lack of academic success or when offered help. She may have a learning disability like "learned helplessness," believing nothing she does will make any difference. This can result in hostility to any suggestion that is intended to help her succeed.

- She is not completing her work. One hypothesis is that she does not understand directions, has difficulty organizing her time, or wants to fail.

Score of 1

The response presents one aspect of her behavior that they might review and suggests one hypothesis about her as a learner, such as those presented in score point 2, or presents two aspects of her behavior they might review but does not suggest a hypothesis about either of them.

Score of 0

The response fails to address the question, presents aspects of her behavior that are not supported by the case and/or inappropriate hypotheses, or is vague.

Response that would receive a score of 2.

There are several aspect of Pauline's behavior that they might discuss that suggest hypotheses about her as a learner. First, she seems very disengaged from class, staring out the window when she should be working. She may have some kind of emotional problem marked by an intense dislike of the classroom, and may need to retreat from any situation she finds uncomfortable. Second, she is very hostile. She may be having emotional problems at home, at school, or in some other area of her life that are causing her to be angry at everyone.

Commentary on the above response

The response presents two appropriate aspects of her behavior for consideration, and for each, suggests a hypothesis they might explore to learn more about Pauline as a learner. The response receives full credit.

Response that would receive a score of 1.

She is not completing her work. In fact, the teacher notes that she "has completed few of the assignments so far with any success." Pauline is probably just one of many students who do not complete their assignments. This seems to be a major problem with many students at this state of their education. The hypothesis to investigate is that she has just given up, that she has decided she can't succeed no matter what she does, so she might as well not try.

Commentary on the above response

The response presents one appropriate aspect of her behavior for consideration, and a hypothesis they might explore related to this behavior. However, it does not present two aspects of her behavior with a hypothesis for each, so it receives partial credit.

Response that would receive a score of 0.

I don't think Mr. Payton and the counselor should meddle with Pauline's life. She is obviously having a lot of problems, and if they begin to investigate things that she may feel are very personal, they may only make matters worse. Usually, Pauline and students like her go through these stages, but outgrow them.

Commentary on the above response

The response does not address the question, but rather argues with its premise. Responses that argue with the question rather than responding to it receive no credit.

This completes the chapters of the study guide focusing on case studies and constructed-response questions. We suggest you now move on to strategies, advice, and practice on multiple-choice questions.

Chapter 8
Don't Be Defeated by Multiple-Choice Questions

▶   ▶   ▶   ▶   ▶   ▶   ▶   ▶   ▶   ▶   ▶   ▶

Why the Multiple-Choice Tests Take Time

When you answer the practice questions, you will see that there are very few simple identification questions. For the Praxis assessment, you are not likely to be asked, "Which of the following authors wrote *Moby-Dick*?" This is because when The Praxis Series™ Assessments were first being developed by teachers and teacher educators across the country, almost all agreed that prospective teachers should be able to analyze situations, synthesize material, and apply knowledge to specific examples. They believed that teachers should be able to think as well as to recall specific facts, figures, or formulas. Consequently, you will find that you are being asked to *think* and to *solve* problems on your test. Such activity takes more time than simply answering identification questions.

In addition, questions that require you to analyze situations, synthesize material, and apply knowledge are usually longer than simple identification questions. The exercises in The Praxis Series tests often present you with something to read (a case study, a sample of student work, a chart or graph) and ask you questions based on your reading. Strong reading skills are required, and you must read carefully. Both on this test and as a teacher, you will need to process and use what you read efficiently.

If you know your reading skills are not strong, you may want to take a reading course. College campuses have reading labs that can help you strengthen your reading skills.

Understanding Multiple-Choice Questions

You will probably notice that the syntax or word order in multiple-choice questions is different from the word order you're used to seeing in ordinary material that you read, such as newspapers or textbooks. One of the reasons for this difference is that many such questions contain the phrase "which of the following."

The purpose of the phrase "which of the following" is to limit your choice of answers only to the list given. For example, look at this question.

> Which of the following is a flavor made from beans?
>
> (A) Strawberry
> (B) Cherry
> (C) Vanilla
> (D) Mint

You may know that chocolate and coffee are flavors made from beans also, but they are not listed, and the question asks you to select from among the list that follows ("which of the following"). So the answer has to be the only bean-derived flavor in the list: vanilla.

Notice that the answer can be substituted for the phrase "which of the following." In the question above, you could insert "vanilla" for "which of the following" and have the sentence "Vanilla is a flavor made from beans." Sometimes it helps to cross out "which of the following" and insert the various choices. You may want to give this technique a try as you answer various multiple-choice questions in the practice test.

Looking carefully at the "which of the following" phrase helps you to focus on what the question is asking you to find and on the answer choices. In the simple example above, all of the answer choices are flavors. Your job is to decide which of the flavors is the one made from beans.

The vanilla bean question is pretty straightforward. But the phrase "which of the following" can also be found in more challenging questions. Look at this question:

> Some teachers require their students to give oral book reports. Which of the following is the best rationale for using oral book reports to motivate students to read?
>
> (A)   They provide students with practice in making formal presentations before a group.
> (B)   They show that students have read the books and know the plots.
> (C)   They require students to analyze every book they read.
> (D)   They encourage students to share their reading experiences with others.

The placement of "which of the following" tells you that the list of choices is a list of "rationales." What are you supposed to find as an answer? You are supposed to find the choice that describes a motivating factor inherent in the activity of giving an oral book report.

Sometimes it helps to put the question in your own words. Here, you could paraphrase the question as "Why is an oral book report something that would help make a student want to read?" (The answer is (D).)

You may find that it helps you to circle or underline each of the critical details of the question in your test book so that you don't miss any of them. It's only by looking at all parts of the question carefully that you will have all of the information you need to answer it.

Circle or underline the critical parts of what is being asked in this question.

> A highly visual learner is most likely to learn the key concepts in a chapter on the human skeletal system through which of the following activities?
>
> (A)   Taking careful notes when the teacher reviews the chapter
> (B)   Re-reading the chapter at home with more privacy
> (C)   Discussing the key concepts with fellow students in a small group
> (D)   Drawing a web diagram of the key concepts presented in the chapter

Here is one possible way you may have annotated the question:

> A <u>highly visual learner</u> is most likely to learn the <u>key concepts</u> in a chapter on the <u>human skeletal system</u> through which of the following (activities)?
>
> (A)   Taking careful notes when the teacher reviews the chapter
> (B)   Re-reading the chapter at home with more privacy
> (C)   Discussing the key concepts with fellow students in a small group
> (D)   Drawing a web diagram of the key concepts presented in the chapter

After spending a minute with the question, you can probably see that you are being asked to recognize an activity that would help a visual learner consolidate his or her knowledge of the human skeletal system. (The answer is (D).) The important thing is understanding what the question is asking. With enough practice, you should be able to determine what any question is asking. Knowing the answer is, of course, a different matter, but you have to understand a question before you can answer it.

It takes even more work to understand "which of the following" questions when there are more words in them. Questions that require application or interpretation invariably require extra reading.

Consider this question

During a visit to a second-grade classroom, a student teacher observed a child spending the time allotted for a worksheet either looking out the window or doodling on his paper. When the student teacher asked the child if he needed help on the assignment, he said no. When asked why he wasn't doing it, he pointed to another student and said, "She does all her work fast and when she's done, she gets more work."

The boy's reaction suggests that which of the following statements is true about his classroom?

(A)   A routine has been established for students who are having trouble finishing an assignment to ask the teacher for assistance.

(B)   A routine for rewarding students who finish work promptly is not in place.

(C)   Students must work alone on seatwork, without consulting other students.

(D)   Students who finish work before the whole class is finished must not interrupt the students who are still working.

Given the placement of the phrase "which of the following," you can tell that the list of answer choices is a list of statements that describe a classroom. You are supposed to pick the statement that is most consistent with the boy's reaction.

Being able to select the right answer depends on your understanding of the situation given. Make sure you read the situation carefully so that you understand the issue being illustrated. In this case, the boy *could* finish his work but does not, because he does not want extra work.

(The correct answer is (B).)

Understanding questions containing "NOT," "LEAST," or "EXCEPT"

In addition to "which of the following" and details that must be understood, the words "NOT," "EXCEPT," and "LEAST" often make comprehension of test questions more difficult. These words are always capitalized when they appear in The Praxis Series test questions, but they are easily (and frequently) overlooked.

For the following test question, determine what kind of answer you need and what the details of the question are.

All of the following are instructionally sound reasons for using a concept map EXCEPT

(A)   to assess students' progress on writing a report

(B)   to gauge prior knowledge of a topic

(C)   to serve as a review before a test

(D)   to function as an end-of-lesson, chapter, or unit evaluation

You're looking for the reason that is NOT a relevant rationale for using a concept map. (A) is the answer —all of the other choices *are* sound reasons for using a concept map.

Tip

It's easy to get confused while you're processing the information to answer a question with a LEAST, NOT, or EXCEPT in the question. If you treat the word "LEAST," "NOT," or "EXCEPT" as one of the details you must satisfy, you have a better chance of understanding what the question is asking. Therefore, when you check your answer, make "LEAST," "NOT," or "EXCEPT" one of the details you check for.

Here's an example of a question that uses the word "LEAST."

An elementary school teacher wants students to become life-long readers. Which of the following is LEAST likely to help achieve that goal?

(A)   Giving students a choice of books to read for a book report

(B)   Providing students with time each day to read a book of their own choosing

(C)   Assigning each student an author about whom he or she is to read a biography

(D)   Reading aloud books that are interesting and exciting, even if some are above grade level

You're looking for the activity with the *smallest* chance of making students enthusiastic about reading. The answer is (C).

Again, the key to answering questions with LEAST is remembering that you are looking for the smallest or *lowest* degree as your correct answer. For questions with EXCEPT or NOT, you are looking for the *incorrect* choice as your correct answer.

Be Familiar with Multiple-Choice Question Types

You will probably see more than one question format on a multiple-choice test. Here are examples of some of the more common question formats.

1.   **Complete the statement.** In this type of question, you are given an incomplete statement. You must select the choice that will make the completed statement correct.

The concept of the placement of students in the "least restrictive" educational environment developed as a result of efforts to

(A)   equalize educational opportunities for females and minorities

(B)   normalize the lives of those children with disabilities who were being educated in isolation from their peers

(C)   obtain increased federal funding for the noneducational support of children living in poverty

(D)   reduce the overall costs of educating students with special needs

To check your answer, reread the question and add your answer choice at the end. Be sure that your choice best completes the sentence. The correct answer is (B).

2. **Which of the following.** This question type is discussed in detail in a previous section. Also discussed above are strategies for helping you understand what the question is asking and for helping you sort out the details in the question that will help you make the correct choice.

3. **Roman numeral choices.** This format is used when there can be more than one correct answer in the list. Consider the following example.

A third-grade class is learning about the 50 states of the United States and their capitals. The teacher uses a variety of independent, whole-class, and at-home learning activities to meet the objectives of the unit. After testing the students on all of the objectives, the teacher compares individual student performance to the performance of the other students in the class.

The evaluation described above is best characterized as which of the following?

    I.   Formative
   II.   Summative
 III.   Norm-referenced
 IV.   Criterion-referenced

(A)   I and III
(B)   I and IV
(C)   II and III
(D)   II and IV

One useful strategy in this type of question is to assess each possible roman numeral answer before looking at the lettered answer choices. In the question above, the teacher is testing the "sum" of the objectives, making it a "summative" assessment, and the teacher compares individual results to the rest of the class, making it a "norm-referenced" evaluation. So the answer is (C).

4. **Questions with LEAST, EXCEPT, or NOT.** This question type is discussed at length above. It asks you to select the choice that doesn't fit. You must be very careful with this question type, because it's easy to forget that you're selecting the negative. This question type is used in situations in which there are several good solutions or ways to approach something, but also a clearly wrong way to do something.

5. **Questions about graphs, tables, or reading passages.** The important thing to keep in mind when answering questions about tables, graphs, or reading passages is to answer the question that is asked. In the case of a graph or table, you should consider reading the questions first, and then looking at the graph or table in light of the questions you have to answer. In the case of a reading passage, you might want to go ahead and read the passage, marking places you think are important, and then answer the questions.

Look at this example

A science teacher plans to teach a health education unit on nutrition. Students are divided into heterogeneous groups of four members. Each group is assigned a different section of the same article to read, to summarize, and to become ready to teach to fellow students. Students then regroup, with members of the new groups representing all four sections. Each member of a new group teaches the other three group members about his or her section of the article.

Which of the following teaching and learning strategies is best described by this exercise?

(A) Demonstration

(B) Portfolio

(C) Jigsaw method

(D) Think-pair-share

First, read through the scenario. When you get to the question, if you can't answer it right away, go back to the passage and focus on the method of grouping students and the kind of activity that is taking place. (The correct answer is (C).)

Here is another example

Literature should not be "used" in the classroom but should be "received" by children. We want students to view literature not simply as a resource, a thing to practice, but as an experience to be entered into, to be shared and contemplated. This is what we must teach children, by discovery, that literature is.

Which of the following best characterizes the view presented in the passage?

(A) It is an argument in favor of skill-based reading programs.

(B) It is an argument in favor of allowing teachers to select the reading series used in their classrooms.

(C) It is an argument embodying many of the principles of whole-language instructional approaches.

(D) It is an argument against a metacognitive approach to reading instruction.

As with the question above, the best way to approach this question would be to read through the passage first. If you cannot answer the question immediately, go back and re-read the passage, focusing on the argument being made by the author. (The answer is (C).)

6. **Other Formats.** New question formats are developed from time to time in order to find new ways of assessing knowledge with multiple-choice questions. If you see a format with which you are not familiar, read the directions carefully. Then read and approach the question the way you would any other question, asking yourself what you are supposed to be looking for, and what details are given in the question that help you find the answer.

Useful Facts About the Test

1. **You can answer the questions in any order.** You can go through the questions from beginning to end, as many test takers do, or you can create your own path. Perhaps you will want to answer questions in your strongest area of knowledge first and then move from your strengths to your weaker areas. There is no right or wrong way. Use the approach that works for you.

2. **There are no trick questions on the test.** You don't have to find any hidden meanings or worry about trick wording. All of the questions on the test ask about subject matter knowledge in a straightforward manner.

3. **Don't worry about answer patterns.** There is one myth that says that answers on multiple-choice tests follow patterns. There is another myth that there will never be more than two questions with the same lettered answer following each other. There is no truth to either of these myths. Select the answer you think is correct, based on your knowledge of the subject.

4. **There is no penalty for guessing.** The multiple-choice part of your test score is based on the number of correct answers you have, and

incorrect answers are not counted against you. When you don't know the answer to a question, try to eliminate any obviously wrong answers and then guess at the correct one.

5. **It's OK to write in your test booklet.** You can make notes to yourself, mark questions you want to review later, or write anything at all. Your test booklet will be destroyed after you are finished with it, so use it in any way that is helpful to you.

Smart Tips for Taking the Test

1. **Put your answers in the right "bubbles."** It seems obvious, but be sure that you are "bubbling in" the answer to the right question on your answer sheet. You would be surprised at how many candidates fill in a "bubble" without checking to see that the number matches the question they are answering.

2. **Skip the questions you find to be extremely difficult.** There are bound to be some questions that you think are hard. Rather than trying to answer these on your first pass through the test, leave them blank and mark them in your test booklet so that you can come back to them. Pay attention to the time as you answer the rest of the questions on the test and try to finish with 10 or 15 minutes remaining so that you can go back over the questions you left blank. Even if you don't know the answer the second time you read the questions, see if you can narrow down the possible answers, and then guess.

3. **Keep track of the time.** Bring a watch to the test, just in case the clock in the test room is difficult for you to see. You will probably have plenty of time to answer all of the questions, but if you find yourself becoming bogged down in one section, you might decide to move on and come back to that section later.

4. **Read all of the possible answers before selecting one—and then reread the question to be sure the answer you have selected really answers the question being asked.** Remember that a question that contains a phrase like "Which of the following does NOT..." is asking for the one answer that is NOT a correct statement or conclusion.

5. **Check your answers.** If you have extra time left over at the end of the test, look over each question and make sure that you have filled in the "bubble" on the answer sheet as you intended. Many test takers make careless mistakes that could have been corrected if they had checked their answers.

6. **Don't worry about your score when you are taking the test.** No one is expected to answer all of the questions correctly. Your score on this test is not analogous to your score on the SAT, the GRE, or other similar tests. It doesn't matter on this test whether you score very high or barely pass. If you meet the minimum passing scores for your state, and you meet the other requirements of the state for obtaining a teaching license, you will receive a license. Your actual score doesn't matter, as long as it is above the minimum required score. With your score report you will receive a booklet entitled *Understanding Your Praxis Scores,* which lists the passing scores for your state.

Chapter 9
Practice Test—Multiple-Choice

▶ ▶ ▶ ▶ ▶ ▶ ▶ ▶ ▶ ▶ ▶ ▶

Now that you have studied the content topics and have worked through strategies relating to multiple-choice questions, you should take the following practice test. You will probably find it helpful to simulate actual testing conditions, giving yourself about 25 minutes to work on the questions. You can cut out and use the answer sheet provided if you wish.

Keep in mind that the test you take at an actual administration will have different questions. You should not expect the percentage of questions you answer correctly in these practice questions to be exactly the same as when you take the test at an actual administration, since numerous factors affect a person's performance in any given testing situation.

When you have finished the practice questions, you can score your answers and read the explanations of the best answer choices in chapter 10.

THE **PRAXIS**
S E R I E S
Professional Assessments for Beginning Teachers ®

TEST NAME:

Principles of Learning and Teaching

Practice Multiple-Choice Questions

Time—25 minutes

26 Multiple-Choice Questions

PRINCIPLES OF LEARNING AND TEACHING

Answer Sheet O

THE PRAXIS SERIES
Professional Assessments for Beginning Teachers

ETS

DO NOT USE INK

Use only a pencil with soft black lead (No. 2 or HB) to complete this answer sheet.
Be sure to fill in completely the oval that corresponds to the proper letter or number.
Completely erase any errors or stray marks.

1. NAME
Enter your last name and first initial.
Omit spaces, hyphens, apostrophes, etc.

Last Name (first 6 letters)

F I

(A) through (Z) ovals

2.

YOUR NAME: (Print)
Last Name (Family or Surname)   First Name (Given)   M. I.

MAILING ADDRESS: (Print)
P.O. Box or Street Address
Apt. # (if any)

City
State or Province

Country
Zip or Postal Code

TELEPHONE NUMBER:
Home   Business

SIGNATURE:

TEST DATE:

3. DATE OF BIRTH

Month	Day
Jan.	
Feb.	
Mar.	
April	
May	
June	
July	
Aug.	
Sept.	
Oct.	
Nov.	
Dec.	

4. SOCIAL SECURITY NUMBER

(0)(1)(2)(3)(4)(5)(6)(7)(8)(9)

5. CANDIDATE ID NUMBER

(0)(1)(2)(3)(4)(5)(6)(7)(8)(9)

6. TEST CENTER / REPORTING LOCATION

Center Number   Room Number

Center Name

City   State or Province

Country

7. TEST CODE / FORM CODE

(0)(1)(2)(3)(4)(5)(6)(7)(8)(9)

8. TEST BOOK SERIAL NUMBER

9. TEST FORM

0
1

PAGE 2

CASE I

1. Write your response on the appropriate page of the response book.

2. Write your response on the appropriate page of the response book.

3. Write your response on the appropriate page of the response book.

CASE II

4. Write your response on the appropriate page of the response book.

5. Write your response on the appropriate page of the response book.

6. Write your response on the appropriate page of the response book.

7 Ⓐ Ⓑ Ⓒ Ⓓ
8 Ⓐ Ⓑ Ⓒ Ⓓ
9 Ⓐ Ⓑ Ⓒ Ⓓ
10 Ⓐ Ⓑ Ⓒ Ⓓ
11 Ⓐ Ⓑ Ⓒ Ⓓ
12 Ⓐ Ⓑ Ⓒ Ⓓ
13 Ⓐ Ⓑ Ⓒ Ⓓ
14 Ⓐ Ⓑ Ⓒ Ⓓ
15 Ⓐ Ⓑ Ⓒ Ⓓ
16 Ⓐ Ⓑ Ⓒ Ⓓ
17 Ⓐ Ⓑ Ⓒ Ⓓ
18 Ⓐ Ⓑ Ⓒ Ⓓ

CASE III

19. Write your response on the appropriate page of the response book.

20. Write your response on the appropriate page of the response book.

21. Write your response on the appropriate page of the response book.

CASE IV

22. Write your response on the appropriate page of the response book.

23. Write your response on the appropriate page of the response book.

24. Write your response on the appropriate page of the response book.

25 Ⓐ Ⓑ Ⓒ Ⓓ
26 Ⓐ Ⓑ Ⓒ Ⓓ
27 Ⓐ Ⓑ Ⓒ Ⓓ
28 Ⓐ Ⓑ Ⓒ Ⓓ
29 Ⓐ Ⓑ Ⓒ Ⓓ
30 Ⓐ Ⓑ Ⓒ Ⓓ
31 Ⓐ Ⓑ Ⓒ Ⓓ
32 Ⓐ Ⓑ Ⓒ Ⓓ
33 Ⓐ Ⓑ Ⓒ Ⓓ
34 Ⓐ Ⓑ Ⓒ Ⓓ
35 Ⓐ Ⓑ Ⓒ Ⓓ
36 Ⓐ Ⓑ Ⓒ Ⓓ

PRINCIPLES OF LEARNING AND TEACHING

1. In working with her fifth-grade students to develop their literacy skills, Ms. Wood wants to employ a constructivist approach. She could best do this by using which of the following strategies?

    (A) Help them improve their writing by presenting them with effective sentences that they first read aloud and then use as models for their own writing

    (B) Have them read stories and then respond by making connections to their own lives and to other things they have read and then writing their own interpretation of the stories

    (C) Have them analyze the style and structure of a series of sentences and then revise a second set of sentences to match the style and structure of the first set

    (D) Have them work in pairs to revise short pieces of writing, making changes for both technical correctness and vividness of detail

2. Mr. Ruiz, in planning his lessons, wants to base much of his instructional approach on Lev Vygotsky's theory of the "zone of proximal development." In accordance with this theory, which of the following strategies would best support learning for Lea, a 13-year-old girl?

    (A) Having her work alone in a quiet atmosphere where she can access reference material appropriate to her grade level

    (B) Giving her many opportunities for practice, thereby reinforcing the skills and concepts that she has already mastered

    (C) Having her work with another student whose skill and concept levels are slightly more advanced than hers

    (D) Having her use manipulatives and technology that are readily available

3. In having students keep learning logs, Ms. Potter encourages her tenth-grade students to evaluate their own learning and to identify those learning strategies that seem to help them the most. In doing so, she is most likely to develop their ability in which of the following?

    (A) Social learning
    (B) Metacognition
    (C) Transfer
    (D) Discovery learning

4. Mr. Young's middle school students are having difficulty with a project that asks them to keep a notebook in which they record careful, systematic scientific observations and then write two possible hypotheses that could be tested on the basis of the observations. Which of the following theories might best help him understand why so many of his students are having difficulty with the project?

    (A) Erik Erikson's theory on the stages of psychological development
    (B) Jerome Bruner's theory on how information is processed
    (C) Jean Piaget's theory on the stages of cognitive development
    (D) Lev Vygotsky's theory on social learning

Questions 5–8 are based on the following description of a class and the teacher's goals.

Mr. Byrd teaches a seventh-grade English/social studies core class of 26 students.

- For 12 students, English is the second language; they represent five different language groups with a wide range of English fluency.
- Two students are placed in the class on the "least-restrictive environment" provision.
- Four students have been identified as qualifying for the "gifted and talented" program.
- Two students are repeating the class after having failed it the previous year.

Mr. Byrd's goals for the class include:

(1) Students will develop speaking and listening skills, both in formal presentations and informal discussions.

(2) Students will develop skills for working cooperatively and supportively.

(3) Students will develop reading and writing skills within the social studies curriculum.

---

5. Mr. Byrd is working on plans to address his first goal, "Students will develop speaking and listening skills, both in formal presentations and informal discussions." He has decided to begin the class by having pairs of students interview and then introduce each other to the rest of the class. Which of the following has the potential for helping the students for whom English is a second language perform well in this activity?

   (A) Presenting a model of an interview and introduction in which a student from a previous year interviews Mr. Byrd and then introduces him

   (B) Providing a set of written guidelines on conducting an interview and introducing another person

   (C) Having students discuss among themselves what completing the activity successfully will require

   (D) Providing a rubric by which both the interviews and the introductions will be evaluated

Matt is one of the two students in the class under the "least-restrictive environment" provision. Matt has a very limited attention span and says he usually cannot follow what is going on in class. One of the IEP objectives for Matt is "Given a 15–20 minute lecture/oral lesson, Matt will take appropriate notes as judged by the teacher."

6. Which of the following strategies has the best potential to help Matt meet this goal by the end of the year?

   (A) Mr. Byrd grades Matt's notes on lecture/oral lesson material and incorporates the grade into Matt's overall class grade.

   (B) Mr. Byrd allows Matt to tape-record the lecture/oral lesson, rather than taking notes, and then listen to the tape at home to learn the material.

   (C) Mr. Byrd provides Matt with a graphic organizer, or a skeleton outline, of the lecture so Matt can fill in the missing information as it is provided.

   (D) Mr. Byrd seats Matt with a student he says he likes and allows Matt to ask that student questions as the lecture/oral lesson proceeds.

At the end of the first grading period, Mr. Byrd confirms his impression that five of the students for whom English is a second language are receiving failing or near-failing grades in both English and social studies.

7. Mr. Byrd could most effectively begin to address their needs as learners by doing which of the following?

 (A) Placing these students in a special learning group within the class so they can help each other, and allowing the other students to move at the regular place

 (B) Requesting an assessment of the students' oral language abilities, both in their first language and in English

 (C) Providing a differential grading policy for these students that would reward them for whatever efforts they make

 (D) Making sure that the families of these students have a copy of the course outline and copies of textbooks and other materials

In addition to planning instruction to help students meet his second goal, "Students will develop skills for working cooperatively and supportively," Mr. Byrd is also working to meet the district goal "Students will learn in classrooms that celebrate all forms of diversity."

8. Which of the following approaches to cooperative learning has the best potential for helping students achieve both Mr. Byrd's second goal and the district's goal?

 (A) Encourage students to work in self-selected groups for cooperative learning so they can work with others with whom they feel comfortable.

 (B) Assign students to cooperative learning groups in a variety of ways that provide for students of mixed abilities and backgrounds to work together.

 (C) Use a random-selection process for assigning students to cooperative groups, such as having students draw numbers, so that there is no indication of bias or favoritism on Mr. Byrd's part.

 (D) Assign students for whom English is a second language to the same groups so they can help each other, and assign the other students randomly.

Fred is a student in Mr. Hall's tenth-grade class. His records show that he has above-average ability, and he says he wants to succeed in class. However, in Mr. Hall's class his participation and performance on most tasks are unsatisfactory.

9. Which of the following practices would be most appropriate for encouraging Fred?

(A) Assign work to Fred in small steps and give immediate feedback.

(B) Pair Fred with another underachieving student so they can encourage each other.

(C) Establish a clear grading system that assures that each piece of work Fred does receives a grade.

(D) Work with Fred's parents to establish a series of consequences to be administered by the parents if Fred's grades do not improve.

10. Kate and Marc are working in the art center making a bird using paper-towel rolls, Styrofoam, feathers, sequins, scissors, scraps of material, and glue. The children are engaged in which type of play?

(A) Dramatic
(B) Constructive
(C) Exploratory
(D) Parallel

11. Ms. Rivers is developing a lesson for her seventh-grade history class. A colleague has suggested that she use scaffolding to help her students access the information effectively. Which of the following strategies has the best potential to help her use this approach?

(A) Having the students role-play important events from the historical period being studied

(B) Asking students to use reproductions of actual historical documents and artifacts to draw conclusions about causes and effects of certain actions

(C) Having students use study guides as they read material and listen to class lectures

(D) Taking students on a field trip to a relevant historical site or museum and then having them write a first-person account of what they experienced

12. Mr. Rose wants to improve the quality of responses and the level of participation by students during class discussion. Which of the following techniques has the greatest potential for improving the thoughtfulness of students' responses and stimulating wider participation?

(A) Keeping a seating chart on which he keeps a record of each student's participation

(B) Using peer tutoring in which more-able students work with less-able students

(C) Waiting longer between posing a question and calling on students to respond

(D) Giving verbal and visual clues to the kind of response he is seeking

▲○◻▲○◻

13. A 5 year old is given the sequence of shapes above and asked to continue the pattern. The student adds the following:

◻▲

Which of the following questions or statements would be most appropriate for the teacher to pose at this point?

(A) "That is not right. Would you like to try again?"

(B) "Can you tell me why you added those two shapes?"

(C) "There are three parts to the pattern. Do you see them?"

(D) "Let me show you how to continue the pattern."

14. Mr. Wright's principal has encouraged the teachers to use discovery learning when appropriate. Discovery learning would be most appropriately used to help students

(A) understand how to divide by fractions

(B) understand the concept of photosynthesis

(C) learn the rules of correct punctuation

(D) learn the skills involved in a new game

Questions 15–16 are based on the following description of a standardized test score report.

Daryl, a sixth grader, receives a score report from a standardized mathematics test taken by his entire sixth-grade class that includes both a grade-equivalent score and a national percentile rank. Daryl's grade-equivalent score is 8.2. His national percentile rank is 87.

15. Daryl's grade-equivalent score indicates that which of the following is true?

(A) Daryl did as well on his test as an average eighth-grade student in the second month of school would do on an eighth-grade test.

(B) Daryl can do the mathematics expected of an average eighth grader who is in the second month of the school year.

(C) Daryl may well encounter difficulties in the later stages of the eighth-grade mathematics curriculum.

(D) Daryl did as well on this test as an average eighth grader in the second month of school would do on the same test.

16. Daryl's national percentile rank indicates that which of the following is true?

(A) Daryl answered 87% of the questions on the test correctly.

(B) Daryl scored the same as or higher than 87% of the students taking the test.

(C) Daryl scored higher than 13% of the students at his grade level on the test.

(D) Daryl scored in the top 25% of the students in his class.

17. A teacher would get better information from a criterion-referenced test than from a norm-referenced test about which of the following?

    (A) How much each individual student has learned about a particular aspect of the curriculum

    (B) How each individual student's knowledge of a particular aspect of the curriculum compares to that of students across the school district and state

    (C) How each individual student's knowledge of a particular aspect of the curriculum compares to that of a national sample of students at the same age level

    (D) How much of what each student knows about a particular aspect of the curriculum is based on prior knowledge

18. Which of the following describes an informal assessment that a teacher might use to check individual students' understanding of a lesson or unit in progress?

    (A) The teacher has students work in groups of three to solve a problem they have not seen before and keep careful record of their reasoning.

    (B) The teacher has students work in groups of four to solve a problem and has one representative of each group come to the board to write out the group's solution.

    (C) The teacher asks each student to write two sentences that answer a question on a topic the teacher has put on the board midway through the class.

    (D) The teacher facilitates a brief whole-class discussion, eliciting questions from students about a topic.

Questions 19–22 are based on the following passage.

The following passage comes from an article advocating that school leaders take deliberate steps to address the problem of "lack of respect."

The problem of lack of respect in most schools —especially middle and high schools—is profound. Students feel that many of their teachers do not respect them and often do not even respect one another. Most of our schools for older students are cold bureaucracies, not caring communities.

The importance of respect in the classroom is probably obvious to most educators—at least in theory. Most students will not work hard for teachers who they feel do not respect them. And they will not try new things or take risks in classrooms where sarcastic comments are tolerated —or worse, modeled—by teachers.

Adult learning and dialogue are similarly inhibited by lack of respect. Younger teachers are often cowed into silence by the snide comments of their older peers in faculty meetings and lunchrooms. Just one or two cynical teachers can psychologically dominate an entire building and so cut off all meaningful conversation about school improvement. A strong educational leader makes clear that the creation of a respectful environment for both students and adults is nonnegotiable and is everyone's responsibility. Incivility is not tolerated from anyone. Conducting student focus groups and then holding small-group conversations about behaviors of concern and behaviors to be encouraged—both adult and student—is often an important starting point. New peer and school norms, or core values, result from such discussions.

Once a safer, more respectful environment has been established in a school, leaders can create teacher teams, suggest meaningful tasks or topics for them to pursue, and set up regular weekly times for discussions. Just as students learn social skills, or "emotional intelligence," through group work, so too do teachers learn how to work more collaboratively through regular problem-solving discussions in small groups. Gradually, the sense of isolation and preference for autonomy give way to pride in the accomplishments of a team—in making more of a difference for students. Over time, teacher groups progress from discussions of curriculum and student work to visiting one another's classes and, finally, to offering critiques of teaching.

19. It can be inferred from the passage that the author believes that which of the following is an important factor in secondary students' motivation to participate actively in learning new things?

   (A) The connections the teacher makes between the topics studied in class and students' own interests

   (B) How much the teacher encourages student-to-student discussion of topics relevant to the class and to the school

   (C) The way the teacher responds to students' attempts to answer questions and speculate about topics in class

   (D) The degree to which teachers in the school share information with each other about students and collaborate in planning instruction

20. Offering critiques of each other's teaching is mentioned in the final sentence of this passage as the culminating activity in a sequence of collaborative collegial work among teachers. It can be inferred that the author places it last in the sequence for which of the following reasons?

    (A) It is more controversial than discussing curriculum and instructional resources.

    (B) Only the most experienced teachers can participate in this kind of collegial activity.

    (C) It requires that the principal be part of the group that visits classrooms and critiques teaching.

    (D) It demands higher levels of social and emotional skills than any other collaborative activity.

21. Which of the following best represents the author's view of the most important role of a school leader in creating a respectful environment?

    (A) To enforce rules of conduct regardless of the student's or teacher's position in the school

    (B) To respond personally to every student complaint about teachers' lack of respect

    (C) To encourage teacher teams to work collaboratively on important issues

    (D) To establish student focus groups to decide on the kinds of rules the school should adopt

22. The passage suggests that which of the following topics would be appropriate for a student focus group in a school that was committed to creating a respectful environment?

    (A) Are there too many rules and regulations for student conduct at this school?

    (B) What kinds of rules and procedures do we need to create at this school to ensure that everyone is physically safe at all times?

    (C) What do you consider to be some of the signs of disrespect for students that are routinely exhibited by teachers and other adults at this school?

    (D) What are the most important tasks for collaborative teams of teachers to work on for the benefit of the whole school?

Questions 23–26 are based on the following passages.

The following passages are taken from a debate about the advantages and disadvantages of a constructivist approach to teaching.

Why constructivist approaches are effective

The point of constructivist instruction is to have students reflect on their questions about new concepts in order to uncover their misconceptions. If a student cannot reason out the answer, this indicates a conceptual problem that the teacher needs to address. It takes more than content-related professional expertise to be a "guide on the side" in this process. Constructivist teaching focuses not on what the teacher knows, but on what and how the student learns. Expertise is focused on teaching students how to derive answers, not on giving them the answers. This means that a constructivist approach to teaching must respond to multiple different learning methods and use multiple approaches to content. It is a myth that constructivist teaching never requires students to memorize, to drill, to listen to a teacher explain, or to watch a teacher model problem-solving of various kinds. What constructivist approaches take advantage of is a basic truth about human cognition: we all make sense of new information in terms of what we already know or think we know. And each of us must process new information in our own context and experience to make it part of what we really know.

Why constructivist approaches are misguided

The theory of constructivism is appealing for a variety of reasons—especially for its emphasis on direct student engagement in learning. However, as they are implemented, constructivist approaches to teaching often treat memorization, direct instruction,

or even open expression of teacher expertise as forbidden. This demotion of the teacher to some sort of friendly facilitator is dangerous, especially in an era in which there is an unprecedented number of teachers teaching out of their fields of expertise. The focus of attention needs to be on how much teachers know about the content being taught.

Students need someone to lead them through the quagmire of propaganda and misinformation that they confront daily. Students need a teacher who loves the subject and has enough knowledge to act as an intellectual authority when a little direction is needed. Students need a teacher who does not settle for minimal effort but encourages original thinking and provides substantive intellectual challenge.

23. The author of the first passage asserts that it takes more than content expertise to implement constructivist teaching. The author would be most likely to choose which of the following as an example of the kind of expertise referred to?

(A) The teacher designs a pre-unit assessment that effectively and accurately indicates students' understanding of the knowledge needed for the class to learn the next unit.

(B) The teacher assesses student understanding of a new concept and then provides some students with a model of the correct strategy to solve new problems and others with a series of new problems to work on, on their own.

(C) The teacher's sequence of lessons indicates a deep understanding of the structure of the content area and the necessary connections among its parts.

(D) The teacher uses individual student portfolios to document learning over time and to reward progress for each individual student, considering the starting point of the student's knowledge.

24. It can be inferred that the author of the first passage would find which of the following classrooms LEAST likely to be constructivist in its approach?

    (A) A classroom in which all new topics are introduced using a set procedure for presentation, questions, and student problem-solving

    (B) A classroom in which structured teacher-led discussions of content follow every introduction of new material

    (C) A classroom in which students work at least 50 percent of the time in structured cooperative groups

    (D) A classroom in which teacher-delivered lectures take up about 80 percent of all class time

25. The first passage suggests that reflection on which of the following after a lesson is an essential element in constructivist teaching?

    (A) The extent to which the teacher's knowledge of the content of the lesson was adequate to meet students' curiosity about the topic

    (B) The differences between what actually took place and what the teacher planned

    (C) The variety of misconceptions and barriers to understanding revealed by students' responses to the lesson

    (D) The range of cognitive processes activated by the activities included in the lesson design and implementation

26. The author of the second passage would regard which of the following teacher behaviors as essential for supporting student learning?

    (A) Avoiding lecture and memorization

    (B) Allowing students to figure out complex problems without the teacher's intervention

    (C) Emphasizing process rather than content knowledge

    (D) Directly guiding students' thinking on particular topics

Chapter 10

**Right Answers and Explanations for the
Practice Multiple-Choice Questions**

► ► ► ► ► ► ► ► ► ► ► ►

Now that you have answered all of the practice questions, you can check your work. Compare your answers with the correct answers in the table below.

Question Number	Correct Answer	Content Category
1	B	Student Development and the Learning Process
2	C	Student Development and the Learning Process
3	B	Student Development and the Learning Process
4	C	Student Development and the Learning Process
5	A	Students as Diverse Learners
6	C	Students as Diverse Learners
7	B	Students as Diverse Learners
8	B	Students as Diverse Learners
9	A	Student Motivation and the Learning Environment
10	B	Instructional Strategies
11	C	Instructional Strategies
12	C	Instructional Strategies

Question Number	Correct Answer	Content Category
13	B	Planning Instruction
14	D	Planning Instruction
15	D	Assessment Strategies
16	B	Assessment Strategies
17	A	Assessment Strategies
18	C	Assessment Strategies
19	C	The Reflective Practioner
20	D	The Reflective Practioner
21	A	The Reflective Practioner
22	C	The Reflective Practioner
23	D	The Reflective Practioner
24	D	The Reflective Practioner
25	C	The Reflective Practioner
26	D	The Reflective Practioner

Explanations of Right Answers

1. This question asks you to recognize the most effective application of the learning theory that proposes that students construct understanding based on their own experiences. Connecting the new stories students read to other things they have read in the past and to their experiences and thoughts about these experiences allows them to build on their current knowledge and understanding. Also, the teacher's goal is to develop the students' overall literacy skills, not just writing skills. The correct answer, therefore, is (B).

2. This question asks you to apply your knowledge of Vygotsky's theory of the "zone of proximal development," which states that instruction is most effective when the level of expectation is slightly ahead of the student's current level of understanding. Vygotsky believed that this "zone of proximal development" was most effectively used to advance student learning when mentoring assistance from a knowledgeable adult or more advanced peer accompanied the instruction. The correct answer, therefore, is (C).

3. This question asks you to recognize the learning process that enables students to identify their own learning styles and evaluate their progress. Metacognition is the intellectual process that enables an individual to step back from a particular learning experience and think about his or her ways of learning new things, preferred and most successful methods of learning, and strategies for most effectively using this knowledge in new learning situations. The use of learning logs represents an important way of having students reflect on their thinking and on how they process new information. The correct answer, therefore, is (B).

4. This question asks you to apply your understanding of the basic concepts of several prominent learning theories. Jean Piaget's work supported a "stage theory" of cognitive development in which children progress from completely physical and tactile methods of understanding the environment and experience (the sensorimotor stage) to methods of understanding that allow them to understand abstract explanations and generalizations across many different kinds of experiences (the formal operational stage). Piaget's classification of stages of developmental readiness suggests that these students may not yet have reached the readiness level to move from concrete observations (concrete operational) to abstract hypotheses (formal operational). The correct answer, therefore, is (C).

5. This question asks you to identify a strategy to support the learning of students for whom English is a second language by realizing that previous experiences and cultural differences influence social interactions. In addition, in working with students whose first language is not English, teachers must keep in mind that reading, writing, listening, and speaking are all parts of language learning. Giving directions that depend on a certain level of facility in one of these areas, and then asking students to make the transfer from those directions to performance in another skill area is very demanding. Modeling the interview allows these students to observe a variety of speaking and listening skills and to note cultural differences—for example,

tone of voice and eye contact. The instructional objective is congruent with the method used to deliver the directions. The correct answer, therefore, is (A).

6. This question asks you to identify an instructional strategy that provides the student with a clearly structured activity to keep him on task to reach the IEP objectives. The information provided about Matt tells you that the strategy the teacher chooses must help Matt in two ways: it must keep his attention from wandering and it must help him to follow what is going on in the lesson. In addition, the strategy needs to provide the teacher with assessment information to use in evaluating the student's progress. The activity is simple enough that it will not distract Matt from the lesson and will not interfere with the learning of other students. The correct answer, therefore, is (C).

7. This question asks you to understand that it is crucial to identify students' levels of abilities and prior knowledge in their own languages in order to effectively plan appropriate instruction and assessment for each student. Without some sense of these students' speaking and listening proficiencies in their first language as well as in English, a teacher cannot adapt instruction and support learning effectively. Oral language proficiency is the most basic starting point for such analysis because classroom instruction and interaction depend on this proficiency as an entry point. The correct answer, therefore, is (B).

8. This question asks you to consider the most effective way a teacher might use cooperative learning to both develop students' skills in

cooperative work and signal consistent support for diversity. Choice (B) expresses the only cooperative learning grouping strategy that assures students the opportunity to develop skills in supportive cooperation and appreciation for diversity in every group. The correct answer, therefore, is (B).

9. This question asks you to apply your knowledge of theories of motivation and behavior (especially Maslow's theory of the hierarchy of needs). We know from the information given that Fred is capable of doing the work and that he wants to succeed. Therefore, some strategy for supporting success in class participation and performance is indicated. Assigning work in small steps and supplying immediate feedback allow the student a greater sense of achievement and more opportunity for positive feedback. This technique also provides the teacher with an opportunity to re-teach material in ways that might ensure Fred's success. The correct answer, therefore, is (A).

10. This question asks you to distinguish among different kinds of play. Because Kate and Mark have a goal in mind and are using the materials to create a specific structure, it would be incorrect to characterize their behavior as simply exploratory play. Additionally, as the two are working together with a shared focus, this would not be considered parallel play. Dramatic play may occur after the students have completed their project, but is not described in the given scenario. The students are constructing a bird sculpture, so this is an example of constructive play. The correct answer, therefore, is (B).

11. This question asks you to apply your knowledge of the instructional strategy of scaffolding. Scaffolding instruction is the strategy a teacher uses to help students understand how new information is organized and how different parts of it are related to each other. Typically, scaffolding involves some tangible aids for connecting and organizing information, such as visual organizers and outlines or content guides that clearly and systematically represent the order of new material. The correct answer, therefore, is (C).

12. This question asks you to identify the concept of "wait time," an instructional technique especially helpful in eliciting responses to higher-level questioning. Providing more time for reflection and using higher-level questioning stimulate students to think at a more complex cognitive level and to provide longer, often unsolicited, more speculative responses. To encourage such responses, teachers must pose questions and then wait for students to think before they respond. The correct answer, therefore, is (C).

13. This question asks you to identify, from the options given, the most appropriate technique for encouraging exploration and problem solving in a young child. The child may see a pattern the teacher does not see and should therefore be asked to explain his or her thinking before the response is judged. The correct answer, therefore, is (B).

14. This question asks you to identify one appropriate use of discovery learning. Discovery learning is an instructional strategy that depends on the teacher's creation of circumstances or situations in which students can induce (or discover) general principles or concepts from their own free exploration of data or experiences. The teacher does not direct instruction in discovery learning, but rather monitors student participation and serves as a resource. The only one of the choices above that offers students a reasonable chance for successful discovery learning of general principles is (D). The correct answer, therefore, is (D).

15. This question asks you to apply your understanding of one particular aspect of standardized test score reporting. A grade-equivalent score is a score that compares the raw score attained on a test by the individual student to the raw score attained by the average student in the norm group for the particular test and then reports the grade and month level of that norm group comparison. In this case, Daryl's raw score was equivalent to the average raw score of all eighth graders in the second month of school who were part of the norm group. The correct answer, therefore, is (D).

16. This question asks you to show your understanding of the meaning of percentile ranking. Percentile rank indicates the percentage of students in a norm group whose scores are exceeded by any specific raw score. In other words, only 13% of the students taking this test scored higher than Daryl. The correct answer, therefore, is (B).

17. This question asks you to recognize the difference between criterion- and norm-referenced tests. Criterion-referenced tests are developed to assess knowledge and understanding of specified standards for learning particular

content. They are designed to enable individual students or groups of students who have studied the same material to assess how much they have learned as compared to the criterion, or standard. A norm group performance is not required for a criterion-referenced test, since the goal is to measure knowledge against a predefined knowledge standard. A good example of a criterion-referenced test is the written test a person must take to get a driver's license in most states. Whether a person passes is not judged in relation to how other applicants performed (which would be norm-referenced) but in relation to an established standard for minimum number correct. The correct answer, therefore, is (A).

18. This question asks you to demonstrate your understanding of the use of informal assessment as a tool to evaluate individual students' understanding. All of the options describe informal assessment strategies, but only one would yield sufficient information for the teacher's evaluation of each person's understanding of material in a lesson or unit. In this situation, asking each student to write briefly allows the teacher to check individual understanding. The correct answer, therefore, is (C).

19. This question asks you to consider a professional question relevant to student motivation. Maslow's theory of needs stresses the importance of self-esteem and dignity to students' mastery needs. The passage indicates that one of the important components in creating an atmosphere of shared respect is how teachers respond to students. The article extends this observation about factors that influence learning from students to new teachers. The correct answer, therefore, is (C).

20. This question asks you to make an inference based on the authors' argument regarding the creation of respectful learning environments in schools. In the final paragraph of the passage, the authors suggest increasingly complex levels of interaction and increasingly ambitious goals for students in a school that is building a respectful environment. The correct answer to this question requires that you recognize the basis for the increases in complexity: social and emotional skills among the participants in the collaborative groups or teams. Only when an atmosphere of trust and respect pervades the teaching and learning process will teachers be willing to invite peers to observe their teaching and offer constructive suggestions. To most teachers, this is a very threatening endeavor, and all that precedes this proposal in the passage sets the stage for this final collaborative process. The correct answer, therefore, is (D).

21. This question asks you to recognize the authors' opinion of the role of a school leader in creating a respectful school environment. The passage says, "A strong educational leader makes clear that the creation of a respectful environment for both students and adults is nonnegotiable and is everyone's responsibility. Incivility is not tolerated from anyone." The correct answer, therefore, is (A).

22. This question asks you to identify a topic that could reasonably be considered appropriate for discussion by a student focus group at a school that was concerned with issues of a respectful environment. The passage says, "Conducting student focus groups and then holding small-group conversations about behaviors of concern and behaviors to be encouraged—both adult and student—is often an important starting point. New peer and school norms, or core values, result from such discussions." Choices (A), (B), and (D) all deal with tangential issues that may or may not be relevant to the specific issue of a respectful environment. The question in (C) simply asks for students' opinions, based on their actual experiences. The correct answer, therefore, is (C).

23. This question asks you to show your understanding of the application of constructivist theory in designing the most effective teaching practices. Constructivist theory places great emphasis on the student as learner and encourages student learning through personal experience and context. In addition, one critical role for the teacher in the constructivist approach is the individualization of instruction, based on each student's particular learning needs. The correct answer, therefore, is (D).

24. This question asks you to evaluate classroom methodology in light of your knowledge of constructivist theory. The author points out that constructivist instruction emphasizes student reflection and reasoning and multiple learning methods and approaches to content. Therefore, classroom instruction dominated by teacher-delivered lectures is least likely to be constructivist. The correct answer, therefore, is (D).

25. This question asks you to apply your understanding of constructivist teaching, which depends on the connection of new information to already learned information or understandings, whether or not they are accurate. The passage says, "The point of constructivist instruction is to have students reflect on their questions about new concepts in order to uncover their misconceptions. If a student cannot reason out the answer, this indicates a conceptual problem that the teacher needs to address." Thus, a consideration of barriers and/or misconceptions in response to the presentation of new material is an essential follow-up to a constructivist lesson. The correct answer, therefore, is (C).

26. This question asks you to identify a teacher behavior that is consistent with the opinions expressed by the second author. The second author maintains that students require teacher guidance and a direct expression of the teacher's expert content knowledge in order to learn most effectively. Choices (A) (avoiding lecturing), (B) (learning without teacher intervention), and (C) (de-emphasis on content knowledge) are not consistent with this approach to teaching. Direct guidance of students' thinking is consistent with the second author's approach. The correct answer, therefore, is (D).

Chapter 11
Are You Ready? Last-Minute Tips

▶ ▶ ▶ ▶ ▶ ▶ ▶ ▶ ▶ ▶ ▶ ▶

Checklist

Complete this checklist to determine whether you're ready to take the test.

❏ Do you know the testing requirements for your teaching field in the state(s) where you plan to teach?

❏ Have you followed all of the test registration procedures?

❏ Do you know the topics that will be covered in each test you plan to take?

❏ Have you reviewed any textbooks, class notes, and course readings that relate to the topics covered?

❏ Do you know how long the test will take and the number of questions it contains? Have you considered how you will pace your work?

❏ Are you familiar with the test directions and the types of questions for the test?

❏ Are you familiar with the recommended test-taking strategies and tips?

❏ Have you practiced by working through the practice test questions at a pace similar to that of an actual test?

❏ If you are repeating a Praxis Series™ Assessment, have you analyzed your previous score report to determine areas where additional study and test preparation could be useful?

The Day of the Test

You should have ended your review a day or two before the actual test date. And many clichés you may have heard about the day of the test are true. You should

- Be well rested

- Take photo identification with you

- Take blue or black ink pens for the constructed-response parts of the test

- Take a supply of well-sharpened #2 pencils (at least three) for the multiple-choice part of the test

- Eat before you take the test

- Wear layered clothing; room temperature may vary

- Be prepared to stand in line to check in or to wait while other test takers are being checked in

You can't control the testing situation, but you can control yourself. Stay calm. The supervisors are well trained and make every effort to provide uniform testing conditions, but don't let it bother you if the test doesn't start exactly on time. You will have the necessary amount of time once it does start.

You can think of preparing for this test as training for an athletic event. Once you've trained, prepared, and rested, give it everything you've got. Good luck.

Appendix A
Study Plan Sheet

Study Plan Sheet

See Chapter 1 for suggestions on using this Study Plan Sheet.

	STUDY PLAN					
Content covered on test	How well do I know the content?	What material do I have for studying this content?	What material do I need for studying this content?	Where could I find the materials I need?	Dates planned for study of content	Dates completed

Appendix B

For More Information

▶ ▶ ▶ ▶ ▶ ▶ ▶ ▶ ▶ ▶ ▶ ▶

Educational Testing Service offers additional information to assist you in preparing for The Praxis Series™ Assessments. *Tests at a Glance* materials and the *Registration Bulletin* are both available without charge (see below to order). You can also obtain more information from our Web site: www.ets.org/praxis.

General Inquiries

Phone: 800-772-9476 or 609-771-7395 (Monday-Friday, 8:00 A.M. to 7:45 P.M., Eastern time)
Fax: 609-771-7906

Extended Time

If you have a learning disability or if English is not your primary language, you can apply to be given more time to take your test. The *Registration Bulletin* tells you how you can qualify for extended time.

Disability Services

Phone: 866-387-8602 or 609-771-7780
Fax: 609-771-7906
TTY (for deaf or hard-of-hearing callers): 609-771-7714

Mailing Address

ETS-The Praxis Series
P.O. Box 6051
Princeton, NJ 08541-6051

Overnight Delivery Address

ETS-The Praxis Series
Distribution Center
225 Phillips Blvd.
P.O. Box 77435
Ewing, NJ 08628-7435

If You Need to Retake the *Principles of Learning and Teaching* Tests

For test codes 0522 (K-6) and 0524 (7-12), you can now order the Praxis Diagnostic Preparation Program if you need to retake the test. The Praxis Diagnostic Preparation Program offers you **detailed, customized feedback** about your performance on the test so that you may better understand your strengths and weaknesses and plan your preparation accordingly. For additional information, please visit our Web site: www.ets.org/praxis.